resuscitating

evangelism

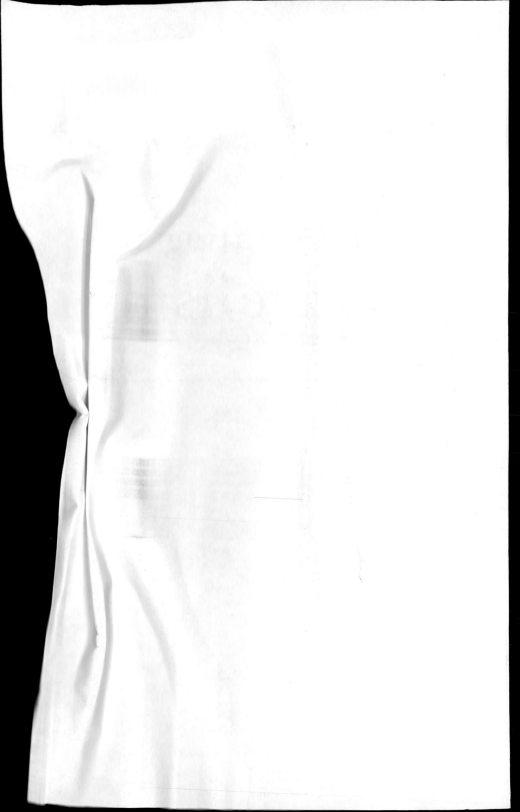

resuscitating
evangelism

JORDAN EASLEY

– – –

ERNEST EASLEY

PUBLISHING
NASHVILLE, TENNESSEE

978-1-5359-4111-2

Published by B&H Publishing Group
Nashville, Tennessee

Dewey Decimal Classification: 269.2
Subject Heading: EVANGELISTIC WORK / WITNESSING /
CHURCH WORK

1 2 3 4 5 6 7 • 23 22 21 20

Contents

Foreword

THERE IS NOT a more urgent need in the local church or in the lives of our pastors, lay leaders, and followers of Christ today than for evangelism. We must get back to sharing the gospel in our personal lives and in our churches. Father and son Ernest and Jordan Easley have done the church a big favor in writing this new book, *Resuscitating Evangelism*. It is practical, personal, and powerful. It is practical in the sense that it takes a look at what works, and gets our finger on the pulse as to where our church is. It helps us get back on our feet in the area of evangelism, addresses some of the reasons we are where we are, and shows us what it will take to see the church on fire for evangelism.

The apostle Paul challenged young Timothy in 2 Timothy 1:6 to fan into flame the gift of God. There is a dire need for our flame to be fanned, and this book is just what we need to see a roaring fire of evangelism, a passion that God places deep in our heart once again to overcome every obstacle that would prevent our churches from being healthy in the area of evangelism.

I have said for years, whatever is important to the pastor will be important to the people. Pastor, read this book, embrace this book, assimilate its truth, and once again, becoming evangelists in your own heart, soul, and life. Then model this ministry before your people and watch your church, once again, enjoy the flames of personal evangelism in your community. It takes a small adjustment in our lives and in our churches to see evangelism among every believer. May that happen in your life and in your church as you read, as you believe, and as you trust God to make these truths a reality.

I can hardly wait to see what God will do as each one of us makes this new commitment.

—Johnny Hunt, senior vice president of North American Mission Board, Evangelism, and Pastoral Leadership

Introduction

EVANGELISM IS NOT dead—at least, not yet. Modern trends and statistics reveal that it's more like a person lying on a hospital bed on life support.

Most Christians today seem to function with a disconnect between what we believe in our head and what we practice with our mouth. We *know* people need the Lord. We *know* lost people need to be saved. But for whatever reason we fail to involve ourselves as part of God's solution to this great problem. It's almost as if something within our soul has been severed, paralyzing us to what we've been called to do.

We as believers have to acknowledge that God isn't okay with this disconnect between our head and our mouth. And if God isn't okay with it, we shouldn't be okay with it either.

This book was written with all followers of Jesus in mind, and it was designed to remind us what Jesus has called us to do and whom Jesus has called us to be. It will also remind us where making disciples truly begins and show us our role in living out the Great Commission in our own context.

Our prayer is that this resource will fan the flame of evangelism in your heart, make you more soul conscious, and resuscitate a passionate desire to see more people saved than ever before.

CHAPTER 1

Checking Our Pulse

THE OLD SAYING *Take two aspirins and call me in the morning* doesn't really apply if you have a fast-growing cancer in your body. You need something far more drastic. But if you don't know the cancer exists, you'll never take the necessary steps to address it. You'll just continue self-medicating, hoping it will eventually go away or fix itself.

To address a problem, we must first become aware of the problem. In order for that to happen, we must intentionally look internally and recognize any warning signs or symptoms that may provide indications that something is wrong. When we as disciples of Jesus Christ take an honest look internally at our hearts, our passions, and our priorities as Christ followers, we'll discover certain things we naturally emphasize and certain things we don't prioritize at all.

What Do We Truly Prioritize?

As a pastor, I will attest—we will never go a week without singing. Nor will we ever go a Sunday without preaching God's Word or passing the offering plate. At our church, we will always have small groups, and we will always have an emphasis on teaching our children about Jesus. We prioritize these things, and as a result, we are consistent in doing them.

Don't get me wrong—all of these things are good. We hold them high because that's what Jesus told us to do. But Jesus told us to do much more than just meet, eat, worship, and teach. Choosing to do a handful of these good things doesn't make you a disciple of Jesus Christ; knowing Jesus, being the person Jesus calls you to be, and living in obedience to His commands are what make you a disciple of Christ. Therefore, if we're going to live the life Jesus called us to live, we must begin prioritizing the things Jesus told us to prioritize.

What Did Jesus Tell Us to Prioritize?

In Mark 16:15, Jesus said, "Go into all the world and preach the gospel to all creation." That is a mandate to the church and therefore should be a priority in our lives. But for many of us, we'd have to admit, who we are and what we do in real life doesn't necessarily match up with who we've been called to be.

When we begin peeling back the layers of our heart and take an honest look internally, we will most likely discover that the *pulse* of our personal evangelism and even the pulse of our corporate evangelism is pretty faint and seems to beat at a slower and slower pace.

Warning Signs and Symptoms

The initial problem is that our personal evangelism pulse doesn't match what Jesus has called us to do. But perhaps the more immediate problem is that the church seems to be in denial. We're like the person who knows something is wrong with his body but refuses to go to the doctor. He continues to live as normal, and all the while the sickness gets worse and worse. The reasons for this may be many, but most likely the attributing factors boil down to two things: complacency and fear.

Complacency and Fear

People who have poor hygiene or don't take care of their body most likely will not prioritize regular visits to the doctor. I recently read a stat that said, "80 percent of Americans avoid preventative care. Further, 9 out of 10 millennials avoid seeing the doctor annually."[1] At first these statistics shocked me, but then it hit me—the reason they don't take care of themselves or prioritize doctors visits is because at this point in their life, they simply don't care enough or see the benefits of taking care of their body.

This is a great example of a complacent attitude. Unfortunately, in this day and time, those who call themselves Christians seem to be more and more complacent. Followers of Christ who do not share their faith may avoid doing so because at their core, they really don't care about other people.

> Followers of Christ who do not share their faith may avoid doing so because at their core, they really don't care about other people.

I know that sounds harsh, but why else would we keep our mouths shut about Jesus when people around us are dying and going to hell? Maybe it's because at this point in our life, we truly don't care. We're complacent.

Or perhaps it has less to do with our apathy and more to do with our fear. Some of us avoid gospel conversations because we're afraid. We're afraid of what it might cost us, or we're afraid of what the outcome might be. We're afraid it won't work, that we won't know all the answers, that we'll lose a friend, or that the whole thing will be embarrassing.

These are the people who avoid going to the doctor because they're afraid of what the doctor might find. We think, *If I avoid going to the doctor, he can't tell me I'm dying. He can't tell me to make adjustments. He can't tell me what*

I'm doing wrong. But that doesn't change the fact that on the inside, there's something wrong! For us as believers, we think, *If I simply avoid sharing the gospel with this person, they won't be able to shut me down, or think I'm weird, or ask me a question I'm unprepared to answer.* Many times we keep our mouths shut because we're afraid. We're afraid because we treasure our own comfort and identity more than our obedience to God.

In Ezekiel 16, we see the results of complacency firsthand with God's children. "Now this was the iniquity of your sister Sodom: She and her daughters had pride, plenty of food, and comfortable security, but didn't support the poor and needy. They were haughty and did detestable acts before me, so I removed them when I saw this" (vv. 49–50).

This passage of Scripture is part of an analogy describing Israel's relationship with God. God had rescued them from their enemies, but in response they turned to other gods. They were too prideful, prosperous, and prone to sin; and as a result, they were "removed" because of their disobedience.

The underlying principle in this passage implies that comfort often leads to apathy and complacency. Israel ignored the poor and needy because they knew that providing aid to these people would have caused them to be inconvenienced in a great way. In short, their inaction was a sin God detested.

I believe this too should be a warning for the church today. The Western church is prosperous and, in many ways, prideful. We have large buildings, big budgets, well-trained church staff members, and countless evangelism and discipleship tools at our disposal. In fact, we have more tools to aid us in fulfilling the Great Commission than ever before, and yet we continue to make excuses for why we don't share Jesus. The poor and needy in today's context not only include those who are physically or monetarily so but also those who are spiritually poor and needy. When we forsake these people and forgo sharing the hope we have in Jesus Christ with them, we are as disobedient to God today as the Israelites were in that day.

When you consider your own pulse for personal evangelism, what do you see? Are you maximizing the moments God gives you and making much of Him, or have you been missing opportunities to share of your salvation? What are the reasons you don't share more often? What are the reasons you may be prone to neglect opportunities to sow seeds of hope in the lost people around you? Is it because you're complacent? Is it because you're afraid?

We've got to look at the answers to these questions as if they are warning signs from the Lord. It's almost as if He's saying, "The complacency you're living with was never a part of My plan for your life! That fear you're experiencing didn't come from Me, but it's keeping you from obeying Me. It's keeping you from living in My will!"

What do the warning signs show you? How will you respond?

Pay Attention to the Warning Signs

A recent study published in the *Harvard Business Review* revealed that the U.S. warning-label system is not accomplishing what it needs to accomplish.[2] The researchers concluded that the label system doesn't do a good job of distinguishing between small risks and large risks. Thus, it becomes easy for the warning labels to cry "wolf" and, as a result, the people that ignore the smaller risks are more likely to ignore the larger risks. That's dangerous because sometimes what may seem like a little problem or a trivial warning is actually something much more significant than we may believe.

When it comes to a lack of evangelism, we tend to disregard it as a real problem most of the time. We miss opportunities to share Christ, and then we justify our disobedience with thoughts like, *Someone else will share with them someday,* or *The timing just wasn't right.* Some may even try to use their theology as an excuse for their disobedience in sharing Christ. Once again, these are all excuses we make that emphasize our underlying belief that *my lack of personal evangelism really isn't that big of a deal.* Before

> A lack of evangelism is always a big deal that always leads to an even bigger problem!

you read another word of this book, you've got to get this: A lack of evangelism is always a big deal that always leads to an even bigger problem! Therefore, we should heed these warnings from the Lord and move forward toward faithfulness.

People who continue to drive their car when their check engine light comes on do so at their own peril. They may not be able to hear or feel that something is wrong, but under the hood a whole lot may be going wrong. The instruction manual to most cars warns the driver to discontinue driving once the check engine light turns on. Unfortunately, when it does, we usually just keep on driving. In much the same way, many believers today complain that their church isn't working or growing, and yet these same people continue to ignore the clear commands in the Bible that tell us we are called by God to fulfill the Great Commission today and share the hope of Jesus with the lost world around us.

Jesus said in Matthew 28:19–20, "Go, therefore, and make disciples of all nations, baptizing them in the name of the Father and of the Son and of the Holy Spirit, teaching them to observe everything I have commanded you." He was clear in His commission to the church. He told us we are to tell everyone in the world about Him, and then we are to baptize those who are saved. He then gave us the responsibility of teaching them God's Word so that they too can do the work of ministry (Eph. 4:11–12), which means we are to equip new disciples not only to walk with Christ but also to share Christ themselves, taking on their place in the mission.

What happens when Jesus' disciples fail to share Jesus? This one truth has been consistent since the book of Acts: churches break down when they disregard God's instructions. Today we see thousands of churches closing their doors every year. Right now we're seeing fewer and fewer people make decisions for Christ and following through with believer's baptism and active church membership. We are living in a world where Christians are looking more and more like the culture around us. These are the real symptoms we're dealing with. So the question is: What are we supposed to do?

David Jeremiah said, "If we have left something or someone, the first step is to remember where we started."[3] If the church would get back to the basics and do what Jesus commanded us to do, I believe we would see a harvest only He could bring.

Current State of Evangelism

On February 21, 2018, the world came to a standstill and watched the funeral of Reverend Billy Graham, who died at the age of ninety-nine. As we watched this beautiful service on the grounds of the Billy Graham Library in Charlotte, North Carolina, we reflected on a life well lived, and we celebrated a job well done. But as I viewed the service, I couldn't help but feel it was more than just the end of one man's life. For me it felt more like the end of an era.

When I was a young man growing up in church, evangelists were considered heroes by many. These were men who packed out stadiums and traveled the globe sharing the hope that only comes through Jesus. They wrote books and provided material and trained laypeople to share their faith. I remember attending tent revivals that would last all week in my hometown, and, over the course of seven days, we would see scores of people stand up to make professions of faith when the evangelist extended the invitation. Those were days where people got excited about salvation, and we longed to see people respond to the invitation.

Fast-forward a few decades, and those days seem to be long gone. Extending an invitation is quickly becoming a thing of the past. Talking about things like "sin," "repentance," "judgment," and "the wrath of God" doesn't exactly go over well in our culture, so we are seeing churches extend anemic gospel presentations—if any—more than ever before. We now live in a day when vocational evangelists are no longer packing out stadiums; in fact, they're struggling to find a place to serve and use their God-given gifts at all. Churches seem to have all but abandoned equipping the saints to share their faith, and, as a result, we're seeing fewer and fewer people baptized every single year.

Is Evangelism on Its Death Bed?

As we stop to check the pulse of evangelism in the modern church, we're clearly experiencing consistent decline. Our trajectory in nearly every evangelism category seems to be stuck in cruise control, heading in the wrong direction. Why is that? Maybe it's due to a shift in focusing too much on social issues. Or maybe we've become too focused on secondary things rather than the primary thing. Some may argue that it's because the Western church has become too complacent because of its prosperity and comfort.

While we've got to be careful generalizing the state of the church, we've also got to realize that some churches take evangelism seriously. However, the participation of many churches is not enough. We've got to come to the realization that God has called all Christ followers and all churches to be fully committed to evangelism. Looking at the current state of evangelism is healthy so that we can be brought to an awareness of reality, but shame on us if we recognize our sickness and then do nothing to address it. We have to ask, *What will it take to turn this around?*

In Ezekiel 37:4–6, God says to the prophet, "Prophesy concerning these bones and say to them: Dry bones, hear the word of the LORD! This is what the Lord GOD says to these bones: I will cause breath to enter you, and you will live. I will put tendons on you, make flesh grow on you, and cover you with skin. I will put breath in you so that you come to life. Then you will know that I am the LORD."

This passage is part of the well-known vision of Ezekiel commonly referred to as "The Valley of Dry Bones." This vision follows God's prophetic announcement in chapter 36, that Israel would be reborn and restored to their land. However, Ezekiel's vision seemed to be disconnected from what was actually going on. Israel was dead as a nation, with no temple, land, or king. Furthermore, the nation was divided. Israel was a mess! But in this vision God had Ezekiel tell the dry bones that God would breathe life into them again. As Ezekiel did so, the bones came to life, flesh developed, breath entered the bodies, and then the bodies stood up to compose an innumerable army. The Israelites thought they were done, but God wanted Ezekiel to tell them a day was coming when they would be made new again.

In the same way, many of us, or perhaps even our churches, may resemble a valley of dry bones today. The life has gone out, our effectiveness has decreased, and our lack of obedience to fulfill the Great Commission has become evident. It's pretty easy to identify with the valley of dry bones at times, but don't forget the underlying principle of this vision. The point Ezekiel made in this text was that God can breathe new life into people who are ready and willing to live for Him! In the same way, God can breath new life into churches that want to live. The current state of evangelism in our hearts and even in our churches may seem sick, or perhaps even dead, but we've got to remember, *our God is a God who brings dead things back to life.* He's a good God who wants us to be maximized here on earth. But as true as that statement may be, we've also got to realize that the devil is real as well, and he is fully committed to doing whatever he has to do in order to prevent that *life* from happening. The devil hates evangelism and will unleash all of his power to prevent it.

> God can breathe new life into people who are ready and willing to live for Him!

God Has Been Patient, but Time Is Short

As you read 2 Peter (the second letter written to various churches in Asia Minor), you see that Peter was anticipating his own death (see 1:14), but he was also challenging believers and encouraging them to grow in their knowledge, faith, and obedience to Christ. In this letter he also warned Christ followers of the false teachers that were present in that day. These people were rejecting the gospel and discouraging other people from believing God's promises in the final days.

In 2 Peter 3:3–9 he wrote,

> Above all, be aware of this: Scoffers will come
> in the last days scoffing and following their

own evil desires, saying, "Where is his 'coming' that he promised? Ever since our ancestors fell asleep, all things continue as they have been since the beginning of creation." They deliberately overlook this: By the word of God the heavens came into being long ago and the earth was brought about from water and through water. Through these the world of that time perished when it was flooded. By the same word, the present heavens and earth are stored up for fire, being kept for the day of judgment and destruction of the ungodly.

Dear friends, don't overlook this one fact: With the Lord one day is like a thousand years, and a thousand years like one day. The Lord does not delay his promise, as some understand delay, but is patient with you, not wanting any to perish but all to come to repentance.

Some believe that in this passage of Scripture, Peter was preaching that time was short, and he was pleading for lost people to repent of their sins. What a powerful message that must have been! But stop for a moment and consider another possibility for a moment. Begin by considering who his intended audience was in this letter. He was writing to the church. He was writing to people who were already following

Jesus; therefore, the intended message to the church may have been a little different. Perhaps the emphasis wasn't intended to be primarily on the unbelievers who needed to repent but rather on the disciples making up the church and their willingness to share the gospel with those unbelievers. The word that sticks out to me is *patient*. In this passage Peter was telling them that God was demonstrating patience with the church.

I believe this message could have been paraphrased along the following lines: "Church, the day of judgment is coming. It's going to happen when God is ready, but in the meantime, just know that God has been patient with you. He's been patient with your effort—or lack of effort—in sharing the gospel, but now it's time for you to get to work because time is short, and I don't want anyone to go to hell. I want everyone to repent and be saved."

Have you ever been waiting in line for a while, daydreaming while standing there, when all of a sudden, something or someone jolts you back to your present state, and you realize the line has moved forward, and now there's a long gap between you and the person ahead of you? The whole time you thought you were the one waiting, but in reality everyone else had been waiting on you! In the same way, we as believers can sometimes find ourselves waiting impatiently for Christ to return, but according to 2 Peter 3:8–9, God is waiting on us. He's waiting for us to obey His Great Commission, and then, He says, that day will come.

What the Trends Tell Us

The current state of evangelism is pretty sad, but our current state doesn't have to be our future reality. Chuck Kelley said, "Here is the thing about bad news. Life brings it to everyone eventually. When it is your turn, do not be afraid of it. Do not avoid or run away from it. Do not ignore it. Do not look for someone to blame for it. Do let it change your behavior, if necessary, so that the bad news can eventually become good news again. It is a call to action more than a call to judgment."[4] That's a good word for the church today! The trends of our past may say one thing, but the trajectory of our future regarding evangelism is fully dependent on our present decisions. What are we going to do next?

> The trends of our past may say one thing, but the trajectory of our future regarding evangelism is fully dependent on our present decisions. What are we going to do next?

If the aforementioned trends continue, the church will continue to lose its effectiveness. Our culture will continue to collapse. Our country will continue to decay and decline. Our families will continue to deteriorate, and more people will die and go to hell. Not only that, but God's Word tells us we will be held accountable for our disobedience and God will remove our lampstand of effectiveness. Revelation 2:5 says, "Remember then how far you have fallen; repent, and do the works you did at first. Otherwise, I will come to you and remove your lampstand from its place, unless you repent."

God used these words to warn the Ephesian church that if they did not repent He would wipe them out as a church.[5] They would cease to exist. Today the original town of Ephesus has no church that can claim it existed two thousand years ago. Apparently, the church did not repent.

The same warning applies to the many local churches that have been called by God to fulfill the Great Commission. Unless they repent of their lack of evangelistic focus, God will cause them to lose their effectiveness and possibly even existence as a church.

What does that look like in our context? If the church continues to ignore evangelism, then it is highly likely that the future of the church will include fewer people being discipled, a lack of cultural effectiveness in the community, the judgment and wrath of God, a lack of freedom in worship, and lost generations who will live without knowing Jesus.

That phrase "Lost Generation" was coined by Ernest Hemingway[6] and was used to describe the generation of young soldiers who had fought bravely during World War I but came back home and felt directionless, purposeless, and disoriented. However, it's also a term that could be used to describe the church of tomorrow if evangelism doesn't become a priority. Without evangelism the church becomes lost and purposeless, and the result will be a spiritually lost generation because no one will have shared with them how they could be saved.

This world needs Jesus, and believe it or not, the world expects followers of Jesus to tell them about Him! Penn Jillette, who makes up half of the famous magic duo Penn and Teller, is more than a famous magician. He's also a well-known atheist. As he was being interviewed one day, he talked about a moment when someone handed him a Bible. Instead of rejecting the Bible, he took it as a nice gesture from someone who was concerned about his life. As he told about this encounter during the interview, the journalists seemed shocked that he would accept such a gift. But Penn went on to say that it doesn't bother him when people share their faith or talk about their God to him. "What does bother me," Penn said, "is when people claim to know Jesus and love Jesus, and yet they don't care enough to tell me about him." He concluded that interview by asking one of the most powerful questions I've ever heard asked. He said, "How much do you have to hate someone to believe that everlasting life is possible and not tell them that?"[7]

Chuck Lawless said,

> So much is at stake here. Millions in North America do not know Jesus. More than 1.6 billion people around the globe have likely never heard of Jesus. Generation after generation of children and young people

are following false religions, deceived by an enemy who wants to keep them in bondage. Families—even Christian families—are falling apart around us. Meanwhile, thousands of churches go through the motions Sunday after Sunday, making little eternal difference. We have increased our numbers significantly since 1950, but we are reaching no more today than we did then. We can only wonder if Satan would say to us what the demon said to the sons of Sceva in Acts 19:15, "Jesus I know, and Paul I recognize—but who are you?"[8]

Don't forget what Jesus told His followers in Matthew 5:13–15: "You are the salt of the earth. But if the salt should lose its taste, how can it be made salty? It's no longer good for anything but to be thrown out and trampled under people's feet. You are the light of the world. A city situated on a hill cannot be hidden. No one lights a lamp and puts it under a basket, but rather on a lampstand, and it gives light for all who are in the house."

Our evangelistic pulse is faint, and yet God's Word is clear. We are called to be salt. We are called to be light. And if we fail to do what God created us to do, if we fail to be who God created us to be, we will become ineffective, "no longer good for anything but to be thrown out and trampled under people's feet." That's not what God wants for you and me; it's not what He wants for His church. He wants us to repent if we have reason to repent. His desire is for us to prioritize the things He's commissioned us to do and to pursue Him like we've never pursued Him before.

CHAPTER 2

Our Source of Strength and Power

MOST OF US hate waiting. It doesn't matter whether we're waiting for our family to get ready for church, waiting in traffic, waiting for the commercials to be over, or waiting for the chips and salsa to be delivered to the table—we hate to wait!

Have you ever found yourself in a season of waiting? Maybe you're waiting to find Mr. or Miss. Right. Perhaps you're waiting for that perfect job opportunity to open up or that promotion you want. Maybe you're waiting for that pregnancy test to finally come up positive, or you're waiting for that much-needed vacation? Do you know what it's like to wait?

When you study the early chapters in the book of Acts, you'll see the disciples of Jesus in a season of waiting. In the first eight verses of chapter 1, we read the final words Jesus ever spoke on planet Earth. Acts 1:4–5 says, "While he was with them, he commanded them not to leave Jerusalem, but to *wait* for the Father's promise. 'Which,' he said, 'you have heard me speak about; for John baptized with water, but you will be baptized with the Holy Spirit in a few days'" (emphasis added).

The Inauguration of Evangelism

For a brief moment in history, God commanded followers of Jesus to wait—not to go, not to share, not to do anything quite yet—just wait. Think about the time line here and the wave of emotions these guys must have been feeling at the time. Jesus had been crucified; they watched Him die. His body was placed in a tomb that was sealed and guarded by Roman soldiers both day and night.

Then a few days later, He appeared once again and was like, "Hey, what's for breakfast?" After convincing them He was alive and showing off some of His scars, then talking to them about the kingdom of God, Jesus told them, "By the way, I'm about to leave, but don't forget about the gift that's coming from my Father. Stay in Jerusalem until you get the gift! Wait for the gift!"

Jesus was referencing the Holy Spirit. He told the disciples to wait in Jerusalem because He was leaving. Do you get that? With Jesus gone, their power was gone. In that moment Jesus was telling them to stay put until they received the gift. This was a promise of power, and Jesus knew it was about to fall on these guys.

This wasn't the first time they had heard Jesus talk about this gift. He actually said that in verse 4: "Wait for the Father's promise, which you have heard me speak about."

One may ask, At what other time had the disciples heard Jesus speak about this gift? One recorded instance was after He had washed the disciples' feet. Jesus went on to say to His disciples in John 14:16–17, "I will ask the Father, and he will give you another Counselor to be with you forever. He is the Spirit of truth. The world is unable to receive him because it doesn't see him nor know him. But you do know him, because he remains with you and will be in you."

He had told the disciples that the gift was coming and said to them, "You do know him, because he remains with you and will be in you." Now, fast-forward to Acts 1 where the resurrected Jesus is reminding them of that conversation, and He's saying, "It's that time right now!" Jesus was telling His disciples, "For the past few years, you've been following Me, but I'm leaving now. Don't worry, because I'm sending the Holy Spirit to be your guide from now on! Don't move until He comes! You don't want to look at the map in your own power and try to decide where to go or what to do. No! Wait for the Holy Spirit! He's going to be your guide and will be in charge of navigating your journey from this point forward."

The message Jesus had for the church was clear. The Holy Spirit is coming, and when He comes, you're going to receive *power*.

"So when they had come together, they asked him, 'Lord, are you restoring the kingdom to Israel at this time?' He said to them: 'It is not for you to know times or periods that the Father has set by his own authority. But you will receive power when the Holy Spirit has come on you, and you will be my witnesses in Jerusalem, in all Judea and Samaria, and to the end of the earth'" (Acts 1:6–8).

> The message Jesus had for the church was clear. The Holy Spirit is coming, and when He comes, you're going to receive *power*.

In that moment the disciples didn't understand fully what it meant to "receive power." They hadn't read the book of Acts because they were living it in real time. In their minds they were most likely thinking, *Finally! We're going to be free from Roman rule! Jesus is about to rule this world, and we're going to be coheirs with Christ in His earthly kingdom!* When this conversation was happening, the disciples were probably daydreaming about a worldly power they were about to be given, but Jesus redirected their focus away from an earthly reign to His spiritual reign. They weren't going to expand the kingdom of Israel through literal military power;

they were going to expand God's kingdom through the message of salvation and Holy Spirit power.

Now we arrive at Acts 1:8, and in this verse we see two main things: words of preparation and words of commission.

Words of Preparation

Jesus prepared the disciples for His work by giving them access to the Holy Spirit. He said, "You will receive power." That phrase is written with a future indicative verb that could be translated something like, "You are *definitely* going to receive power." Jesus told the church the power was coming. He went on to communicate that the power that was coming was coming in the form of a person—the person of the Holy Spirit.

The Holy Spirit is a person. I recently learned that *58 percent of American Christians do not believe the Holy Spirit is a living being.*[1] This is not just harmless, misguided thinking; it is heresy. The Holy Spirit is a person; the one God exists in the three persons of Father, Son, and Spirit. And if you think the Holy Spirit is a "thing" or an "it," you'll always feel like you need more of that thing or more of it. But when we realize the Holy Spirit is a person, it's no longer about *us* getting more of *it*, it's now about the person of the Holy Spirit getting more of us. It's about our yielding and submitting to His leadership in our life. It's about our walking in victory, understanding that we are more than conquerors.

That's what 1 John 4:4 says, "The one who is in you is greater than the one who is in the world." Who's in us? The person of the Holy Spirit is in us, and when He is in you, you have the power Jesus promised His disciples in Acts 1:8.

How did God prepare us to continue what Jesus started? He gave us access to God's power through the person of the Holy Spirit. God sent the Holy Spirit to the disciples because they couldn't do what God needed them to do by themselves. And in the same way, God gives us the Holy Spirit because we as individuals don't have what it takes either.

> God sent the Holy Spirit to the disciples because they couldn't do what God needed them to do by themselves.

Deep-sea divers enter the ocean with oxygen tanks on their backs. You know why? So they can survive in a foreign world. Water isn't our natural habitat, so in order for people to survive under the water, they need to be connected to a life source from our habitat. For us to survive in that world, we need oxygen from our world; and if we get disconnected from the air of our world, we won't last long in that world.

That life source for a Christian living on this planet is the Holy Spirit. Hebrews 13:14 says, "For we do not have an enduring city here; instead, we seek the one to come." We are only visiting here! And in order for us to survive here, and thrive here, and make an impact in this foreign world, we've got to stay connected to a life source from our real home, and that life source is the Holy Spirit.

I grew up in the church, but for whatever reason I always felt like the Holy Spirit was sort of the forgotten person of the Trinity. Don't get me wrong; the Church has always confessed to have Holy Spirit power with our words. But when it comes to our dependence, sometimes, I think we betray our confession because our tendency has always been to rely on our power instead of His power.

We tend to rely on our wisdom and our abilities and our vision instead of His. A. W. Tozer is attributed to have said, "If the Holy Spirit was withdrawn from the church today, 95 percent of what we do would go on and no one would know the difference. If the Holy Spirit had been withdrawn from the New Testament church, 95 percent of what they did would stop, and everybody would know the difference."[2] If that statement is true about the church in America today, it's no wonder we're seeing fewer and fewer people saved.

These were the final words Jesus ever spoke on the earth, and I'd say they are pretty important. He started out with words of preparation. He said, "I've prepared you by giving you access to God's power."

Words of Commission

"You will be my witnesses in Jerusalem, in all Judea and Samaria, and to the end of the earth." These four locations could refer to geographical locations, but I also believe they can refer to people groups. He was saying you now have access to God's power, so go everywhere, talk to everyone, and share the good news! We can do this by the power of the Holy Spirit.

"And if the Spirit of him who raised Jesus from the dead lives in you, then he who raised Christ from the dead will also bring your mortal bodies to life through his Spirit who lives in you" (Rom. 8:11).

God tells us as believers, "I know that what I'm asking you to do seems to be impossible—and guess what? It is impossible. But I'm giving you the Spirit of God, and when He lives inside of you, the impossible becomes possible." In Ephesians 5:18, Paul said, "Don't get drunk with wine, which leads to reckless living, but be filled by the Spirit." He tells the church: don't let anything else fill you up or control you, but be filled with and controlled by the Holy Spirit.

Why the Power of the Holy Spirit Is Necessary in the Church

For Comprehending and Applying God's Word

First Corinthians 2:14–16 tells us that only a person who is full of the Spirit will be able to understand the things of God. Charles Stanley said, "The Holy Spirit knows the thoughts of God. And the Holy Spirit imparts that knowledge to believers. The Holy Spirit, then, is not a simple and impersonal force. He has knowledge, and He has the power to impart that knowledge."[3]

In other words, without the Spirit's revealing power, we will interpret God's Word in a shallow, temporal, and selfish way; but with His help we are able to understand and apply His Word. John 14:26 says, "But the Counselor, the Holy Spirit, whom the Father will send in my name, will teach you all things and remind you of everything I have told you."

For Boldness

Without the power of the Holy Spirit, the disciples went back to their jobs. They hid in their homes because they were afraid of the authorities. They were cowards who lacked boldness. But after Pentecost, when their wait was over and the Spirit's power came down on them, nothing could hold them back. They had a boldness to turn the world upside down for God's glory. These were ordinary people who were now empowered to do extraordinary things because they had the power of God within them.

The same is true for Christians today. The Holy Spirit hasn't aged or changed or become less powerful. As the third person of the Trinity, He is the same yesterday, today, and forever (Heb. 13:8). The same Spirit that hovered over the waters in Genesis 1:2 now resides in the hearts of believers today; and when He is present, He gives us boldness to do the things He's commissioned us to do.

Jesus' command for us to take the gospel to the world appears five times in the New Testament (Matt. 28:18–20; Mark 16:15; Luke 24:45–47; John 20:21; Acts 1:8), and He gave this command to individuals. If Jesus commands us to do something, He expects us to do it. So here's what that command should mean to us: if you're a Christian, sharing Jesus with other people is not *optional*. God commands us as individuals to *share*!

> If Jesus commands us to do something, He expects us to do it.

From Ascension to Pentecost

Now let's get back to the time line in Acts 1. Jesus gave words of preparation and told us He was preparing us to do His work by giving us access to the power of God through the person of the Holy Spirit. Next, Jesus gave words of commission and told us that once we've received that power we are to *go* and *share* the good news with everyone in the world. Then we arrive at verse 9, where we're going to see the next thing in the story: the ascension. "After he had said this, he was taken up as they were watching, and a cloud took him out of their sight" (Acts 1:9).

Here's what happened: resurrected Jesus was hanging out with His disciples (He had been for forty days). Then He tells them, I'm going to leave, you're going to wait, and then I'm going to send the Holy Spirit, and you're going to be My witnesses all over the place. *Then* He floated. He literally floated, and like a balloon that was released into the sky, Christ ascended until the watching disciples couldn't see Him anymore.

"While he was going, they were gazing into heaven, and suddenly two men in white clothes stood by them. They said, 'Men of Galilee, why do you stand looking up into heaven? This same Jesus, who has been taken from you into heaven, will come in the same way that you have seen him going into heaven'" (Acts 1:10–11).

Luke tells us that when Jesus floated away, the disciples were "gazing." They were "looking intently." Well, yeah! I'd imagine so! That word *gazing* in the Greek isn't talking about a casual glance. It's talking about a constant and focused gaze. It's referring to a "mouth-opened-up, eyes-bugging-out-of-your-head" kind of look.

Can you imagine that scene? Think about what's happening here. Jesus is talking. Then all of a sudden He's floating, and before too long they couldn't see Him anymore. Then angels appeared and said, "Why are you standing there with your mouth open?" I love what the angels told the disciples: "Yes, Jesus is going to heaven now. He told you this was going to happen. And just in case you are wondering, He's going to come back just like this someday, so get to work and be ready!" Jesus floated into the sky until He was hidden by a cloud. Luke tells us they watched until they couldn't see Him anymore. Some people believe it was a literal cloud. I believe He was hidden in that moment by Shekinah glory, the visible symbol of God's presence. But either way Jesus was gone. He went back to heaven, and the disciples were left there to wait on the Holy Spirit.

Here's an interesting fact you may not know about the ascension of Christ: Jesus had to leave for the Holy Spirit to come. In John 16:7, Jesus said, "Nevertheless, I am telling you the truth. It is for your benefit that I go away, because if I don't go away the Counselor will not come to you. If I go, I will send him to you."

I think Jesus' was saying: "You don't need more than one pilot. When you have one of us, you have all three of us." For years the disciples had been following Jesus. They let Him lead. They looked to Him for the path to take. They let Jesus sit in the driver's seat. When He was preparing to leave, He told the disciples: the Spirit is going to continue what I started in you. But Jesus had to leave for the Holy Spirit to come. "Then they returned to Jerusalem from the Mount of Olives, which is near Jerusalem—a Sabbath day's journey away" (Acts 1:12).

Not long ago I had the privilege to go to Israel, and I stood on top of the Mount of Olives, overlooking the city of Jerusalem. Having had the opportunity to see this firsthand, I can attest that the journey he was referencing was indeed a short walk (about two-thirds of a mile). It's called a "Sabbath day's journey" to show that it was a short walk and Jews could make this journey without having to overextend their energy.

On the Sabbath, if Jews overextend their energy in any way, it's considered a sin. In fact, in the Israeli hotels we stayed in on our trip, there is a "Shabbat elevator" that automatically stops at every floor because they believe pushing an elevator button is considered overextending your energy and is therefore sinful on the Sabbath.

So the disciples, after being sobered by the words of these angels, made a short walk from the Mount of Olives to the room in Jerusalem where they were staying at the time. "When they arrived, they went to the room upstairs where they were staying: Peter, John, James, Andrew, Philip, Thomas, Bartholomew, Matthew, James the son of Alphaeus, Simon the Zealot, and Judas the son of James. They all were continually united in prayer, along with the women, including Mary the mother of Jesus, and his brothers" (Acts 1:13–14).

So Jesus comes to earth and begins His ministry. He claims that He's God in the flesh. Then He dies for the sins of the world. He rises from the grave. He appears for forty days. He proves He's conquered Satan and sin and death and hell and the wrath of God. Then He gives His followers the greatest mission in the history of the world. He promises to send the Holy Spirit. He promises to send God's power. But in the meantime Jesus tells His disciples to wait.

This was a season when the disciples found themselves experiencing life between the ascension and Pentecost. It was a period when the physical presence of the second person of the Trinity had left them and the third person of the Trinity (the Holy Spirit) had not yet arrived. They were literally waiting, and I'm sure there was some excitement in their waiting. I'm sure there was some anticipation in their waiting. They didn't know Pentecost was coming, but they knew that Jesus promised them power and promised to send them a Helper. They knew *something* was coming.

And take note, in that season of waiting, Luke tells us, the disciples did four things: They gathered. They prayed. They unified. They prepared.

As they were waiting, the disciples didn't just go home and twiddle their thumbs. They didn't waste their wait! What did they do?

- They gathered together and had fellowship with one another.
- They prayed and talked to God about specific things.
- They unified as the body of Christ.
- They prepared for the next season.

Jesus told His disciples to wait for what was coming. Now fast-forward ten days. It's been exactly fifty days since Jesus rose from the grave. That day also happened to be the day of a major festival on the Jewish calendar called Pentecost. Pentecost was a huge celebration also known as The Feast of Weeks. It was a festival that celebrated the end of the wheat harvest, and it happened each year on the fiftieth day after Passover. In fact, the word *Pentecost* literally means "fifty."

"When the day of Pentecost had arrived, they were all together in one place" (Acts 2:1).

Notice, after ten days of preparing for the Holy Spirit and praying with one another, the disciples of Christ were *together*. They were in one place, but more importantly, they were also in one accord. There's something to be said about unity in the body of Christ. Here's what we can learn from the book of Acts: God's power doesn't fall on a divided fellowship. When the Holy Spirit came, the Church was together! It's no wonder, for just as Paul said in Ephesians 4:3, we are to make "every effort to keep the unity of the Spirit through the bond of peace." In Acts 2, the disciples of Christ were together, and they were ready!

> God's power doesn't fall on a divided fellowship.

Have you ever been to a surprise birthday party? A party where everybody is in the room except for the birthday boy or birthday girl? The scene at most surprise parties includes all the guests gathering in one place, scattered all over the house, waiting for the arrival, preparing to *welcome* the guest of honor once he or she arrives. Have you been there before? When I read this text, that's the picture that pops into my mind. The disciples were ready for the Holy Spirit to walk into the room. They were ready to receive this power from God.

> Suddenly a sound like that of a violent rushing wind came from heaven, and it filled the whole house where they were staying. They saw tongues like flames of fire that separated and rested on each one of them. (Acts 2:2–3)

All right, things just got real. In these two verses, there are three supernatural incidents that occurred (violent wind, fire, and tongues), and I want us to unpack all three of them.

Violent Wind

This wasn't an actual wind. Rather, verse 2 says, "Suddenly a *sound* like that of a violent rushing wind came from heaven" (emphasis added). So as we read and interpret this verse, our attention needs to be on the noise that sounded like a violent rushing wind.

That Greek word for *wind* (*pneos*) literally means "a torrent like a tornado."[4] So as they're sitting there, the Holy Spirit comes, and when He does, a loud noise, like an approaching tornado, fills the whole house where they are staying. In that moment God turned the volume up, and He made His presence known.

Have you ever been to a Pentecostal Church? I've been a couple times, and let's just say, it's a different kind of experience than what typically happens where I pastor at First Baptist Cleveland, Tennessee, on Sunday mornings. I'm not saying one is right and one is wrong. They're just different. For instance, before the service begins at our church, people are typically just walking around, talking to other people, putting their Bible in their seat so nobody else sits there. That's what we do.

Before the service starts in a Pentecostal Church, people are stretching! When the service starts, they're ready! When it's time to sing, they sing! And they're into it! When the preacher's preaching, the people are preaching back, standing up, screaming, "C'MON!" I'll be honest with you—I love it! I kind of wish some charismatics would rub off on us just a little bit! I wish we'd get a little more excited about Jesus sometimes. I wish we'd make a little more noise in worship every once in a while.

But hear me when I say this: noise itself is not evidence of the Holy Spirit's presence. Sometimes He moves in ways that are *loud* and *public*. But other times He moves in ways that are *quiet* and *private*. The Holy Spirit doesn't come to us and fill us in order to move our bodies or raise our voices. He comes to move our hearts and sanctify our souls. Charles Ryrie said, "Instead of holy laughter, we need holy living. Pep is no substitute for purity. Words of knowledge don't hold a candle to the words of the Bible. Rather than being slain in the Spirit, we need to be filled with the Spirit. Rather than dancing in the Spirit, we are commanded to walk in the Spirit."[5] In other words, much of the time the filling of the Holy Spirit doesn't occur loudly or publicly but through a quiet, daily surrender to the will of God. But when the Holy Spirit showed up at Pentecost, you could hear Him coming.

Fire

Many times when we read about fire in the Bible, we associate it with bad things like hell and the devil. But in the Old Testament the presence of fire was associated with God's presence. For example:

- The burning bush (Exod. 3:2–4)
- The pillar of fire (Exod. 13:21)
- The covenant with Abraham (Gen. 15:17)
- The flame on the altar (Judg. 13:20)

In all of these examples, fire represented the presence of God. In fact, Hebrews 12:29 tells us that "God is a consuming fire." So in Acts 2:3 we read that fire came to rest on each of these disciples. What that means is, the manifest presence of God came to rest on each of these disciples, represented visually by the fire.

Maybe you're wondering, *Why fire? What's the symbolic meaning of fire?* Well, think about it. What does fire do? Fire spreads. It burns. It purges. It illuminates. It warms. It smolders. God was preparing to spread the gospel like a wildfire through these disciples, but before they could accomplish His will, they first needed His power and His fire!

Tongues

Scholars have debated this word for more than a thousand years. They have tried to determine if these were literal tongues of literal fire or if Luke was using this phrase as an idiom to describe what happened that day. The only thing I'm 100 percent certain of is this: when these tongues of fire fell on the disciples that day, God did something amazing. He empowered His people with His Spirit and gave them the ability to share His gospel in many other languages.

If you remember, Jesus told His disciples this was going to happen before He ascended and went to heaven. In Acts 1:5, Jesus said, "For John baptized with water, but you will be baptized with the Holy Spirit in a few days." When the fire fell on them, they were baptized with the Holy Spirit, and now what seemed to be impossible was possible, and they were being prepared to share the good news with *everyone*!

God's timing is interesting, isn't it? You know that while the disciples were in their season of waiting, they wanted to speed up the process. Ten days seems like a long time to wait when you're waiting for something life-changing! Say it's your job to work with cancer patients in the ICU, and God told you in days He was going to give you the cure for cancer. Those ten days would be miserable, wouldn't they? It would be hard to wait for the cure while watching the people around you struggle and die.

That's where the disciples were. They were waiting and praying, and I'm sure those ten days seemed like an eternity. You know they wanted God's power and God's blessing right away. They didn't want to wait. They wanted it NOW! But God knew that ten days later there was an event on the calendar called Pentecost, and the city of Jerusalem would have more than 150,000 visitors from all over the world, and these people needed the gospel!

So, what did God do? He gave the disciples His presence and His power at just the right time.

The Response of the Spirit Filled

> They saw tongues like flames of fire that separated and rested on each one of them. Then they were all filled with the Holy Spirit and began to speak in different tongues, as the Spirit enabled them. (Acts 2:3–4)

Sometimes we read Scriptures like this and we think, *That would be awesome! Why didn't I get the chance to be baptized in the Holy Spirit?* But the truth is, if you know Jesus as your personal Lord and Savior, you have been baptized in the Holy Spirit. Billy Graham once said, "In my own study of Scriptures through the years I have become convinced that there is only one baptism with the Holy Spirit in the life of every believer, and that takes place at the moment of conversion."[6]

You say, *What's the difference between being filled with the Holy Spirit and being baptized in the Holy Spirit?* And the answer is: baptism of the Holy Spirit only takes place once in a person's life. Every true believer is a burning bush. We have the power of God and the presence of God. But there is a difference between being Holy Spirit filled and Holy Spirit indwelt. The Holy Spirit dwells within the life of every believer; He lives there. He's never leaving. The Holy Spirit also *fills* His people, and He *falls* on people. He *fills* us at certain moments in our life as He works in us and through us. But in these verses He *fell* on the early church and gave them gifts for the specific purpose of spreading the gospel. He gave them the ability to communicate with people when it would have been impossible in their own strength and by their own abilities.

Think about what happened when the Holy Spirit fell on those 120 believers:

- They were empowered by God for the purpose of accomplishing His will.
- They spoke in other tongues. That word *tongues* in the Greek is *glossolalia*, and it

refers to other known languages. Those filled with the Spirit that day were able to speak languages they had never learned "as the Spirit enabled them." Moreover, in verse 6 another word for *languages* refers to the specific dialects of the people. So not only were they speaking in one another's languages but their specific dialects.

• The miracle that occurred at Pentecost did not last but was a one-time event. This supernatural incident is different from the spiritual gift of speaking in tongues. This isn't referring to a *"heavenly" language*; it refers to *other known languages* that God allowed them to speak in this season for the purpose of spreading the gospel to the nations.

The Response of the Bystanders

Now there were Jews staying in Jerusalem, devout people from every nation under heaven. When this sound occurred, a crowd came together and was confused because each one heard them speaking in his own language. They were astounded and amazed, saying, "Look, aren't all these who are speaking Galileans? How is it that each of us can hear them in our own native language?" (Acts 2:5–8)

In verses 9–10, Luke continues to list several places around the world that spoke different languages and dialects in that day. Then he continues in verse 11: "'We hear them declaring the magnificent acts of God in our own tongues.' They were all astounded and perplexed, saying to one another, 'What does this mean?' But some sneered and said, 'They're drunk on new wine'" (Acts 2:11–13).

Luke records a variety of reactions from the surrounding audience that day.

- Confused (v. 6). The audience was confused as to why Gentiles were speaking to them in their own language.
- Astounded and amazed (vv. 7, 12)
- Perplexed (v. 12)
- Curious (v. 12). They asked, "What does this mean?"
- Skeptical (v. 13). They thought the believers were drunk.

This is *the moment* when the Holy Spirit showed up, and from that first moment it's been true that everyone on earth will either receive or reject the Holy Spirit. On that day, as the believers shared the gospel in the streets and as Peter boldly preached, more than three thousand people received the Spirit. It was like an explosion of conversion as the gospel was being shared and people were being saved! But at the same time that was happening, others were standing in the corner making fun of these people, calling them crazy, saying Christianity was a joke, and claiming that it didn't make sense. And the same thing that went on in *that* day continues happening *today*. Question: Have you *received* God or have you *rejected* Him?

If you've truly received Him and been saved by Him, then you have also received the gift of the Holy Spirit in your life, just as Jesus promised the disciples in Acts 1:8. And if you do indeed have the Spirit, there should be no more *waiting*. Once you've received His power and His presence, it's time to *go for it*! It's time to go *everywhere*, and it's time to talk to *everyone* about the hope we have in Jesus Christ! These were the last words Jesus ever spoke on planet Earth, and we've got to take them seriously! The Great Commission is more than simply a great suggestion.

> The Great Commission is more than simply a great suggestion.

We must take this command from Jesus seriously and do more than we've ever done and go more than we've ever gone and give more than we've ever given and share more than we've ever shared because that's the Commission, and He's given us the Holy Spirit in order to do just that.

CHAPTER 3

Addressing Malnourishment

ON MY FIRST trip to Haiti, I saw starving children every-where. It was one of the most heartbreaking things I've ever seen. These were just kids, but because of a lack of food and resources, they were skin and bones, never knowing if and when they would eat their next meal. We would show up in a truck with little bags of food, and these children would literally crawl over one another just to receive their portion. It broke my heart to see the desperation that resulted from their malnutrition.

Malnourishment occurs when a body fails to receive the necessary food and nutrients it needs to grow and function in a normal manner. Malnutrition is such an epidemic that it alone is directly responsible for the deaths of more than 300,000 people every single year globally.[1]

Unfortunately, churches also die slow and painful deaths that can be attributed to malnourishment. When the church doesn't receive the proper diet of sound biblical teaching that God has prescribed, the church will feast on unhealthy food that will ultimately lead to its decay.

A Healthy Diet

When I was eighteen years old, I moved to Dallas, Texas, to attend college. Up to that point in my life, I had only had one pastor—my dad—but now I was being thrust into a new season of life where I was going to *choose* what church to become a part of. I remember walking the campus of Dallas Baptist University, asking students and professors alike which church they attended. As I asked that question, I received all kinds of recommendations, suggestions, and advice in return. But there was something strange about the feedback I was receiving. *Every church that was recommended had some kind of label attached to it.*

People would say things like, "You should go here; they have great worship!" or "You should check out this church; they're a discipleship church and go deep in the Word" or "For college students this is the best church because they focus on age-group ministry" or "Check out this church; they are welcoming to everyone, and they are seeing people saved every week." Every church was recommended based on the *one* thing they were known for.

Churches tend to emphasize certain things, and in doing so, they leave others out. Evangelism has become one of those things that are overlooked. Most churches seem to focus on discipleship—focusing primarily on helping those who are already believers grow in their faith—*or* evangelism—focusing primarily on helping those who aren't yet believers hear the gospel—not both. That's probably because most pastors have a natural tendency to lean one way or the other in their gifting and passion. The truth is—we all do the same thing.

Some of us might say, "I'm in the evangelism camp" and point to Mark 16:15, "Go into all the world and preach the gospel to all creation," as a favorite verse. People in this camp say, "I'm an evangelist because Jesus was an evangelist," and if that's you, you're correct.

But others might say, "I'm in the discipleship camp," and their favorite verses are Matthew 28:19–20: "Make disciples of all nations." These individuals believe, "That's the Great Commission, and because of that, I'm in the discipleship camp." People in the discipleship camp say, "I believe in making disciples because Jesus believes in making disciples," and if that's you, you're correct too.

Resulting from this trend, we now have *discipleship-focused* churches, and we also have *seeker-friendly churches*. We have *deep churches*, and we have what some may call *shallow churches*.

The Christian culture we live in has begun labeling congregations of all kinds. That happens because most churches aren't being fed the balanced diet the Lord designed us to have. Instead, we're picking some parts of the Bible to obey and others to ignore. When we lack balance in the church between discipleship and evangelism, the body of Christ will not receive what is needed to function properly and will therefore become malnourished.

The biblical view of evangelism and discipleship does not treat them separately or interchangeably. If we do it God's way, we cannot do one without the other. In other words, there should be no competition between evangelism and discipleship. They are two sides to the same coin.

> There should be no competition between evangelism and discipleship. They are two sides to the same coin.

The devil loves it when we fail to realize that. He loves it when we live in two separate camps, with two separate sets of priorities and two opposing methodologies. He loves when we lack the balance that God intended for us to have, because it puts us in a place of combat rather than a place of cooperation. The devil loves when the church chooses the battlefield over common ground. He loves when we slip into the idea that says, "We're right and they're wrong."

For that reason we've got to work even harder to align ourselves with the "other" camp—because at the end of the day, we're all on the same team. "Preach the gospel to all creation" (Mark 16:15) applies to every follower of Jesus Christ. "Make disciples of all nations . . . teaching them . . ." applies to all of us. So the question then becomes: *What is the common ground both camps can agree on?*

First, all Christ followers are called to make disciples, and making disciples involves evangelism. In fact, the first step of making a disciple is evangelism. When Jesus says, "Baptize them," He's obviously talking about brand-new converts. He's talking about brand-new believers. Evangelism leads to salvation, which is the first step and the foundation of becoming a disciple of Christ.

When people are *anti-evangelistic* in their life or ministry, they are really *anti-Great Commission*. When someone is overly cynical or even overly skeptical of churches that are seeing a movement of God as salvation, at that point their heart becomes antigospel.

Now, the problem comes along when we see baptism as the finish line rather than the starting line. Jesus never said, "Go and make converts." If He did, it would be okay to stop the process once someone was properly recruited, saved, and baptized; but that's not okay by any stretch of the imagination.

Baptism should never be viewed as the *finish line* in our ministry. Baptism should be viewed as the *starting line.*

A second place of agreement is that making disciples involves evangelism 100 percent of the time. If you don't have a strong emphasis on reaching unchurched people and preaching the gospel, giving them the opportunity to respond to Jesus, you aren't really a disciple maker.

Something else we should all agree on is that making disciples involves teaching. The second step in the discipleship process is teaching the Scripture. When Jesus says, "Teaching them to obey," He's talking about believers walking with people. This is a picture of a person walking someone else through the Word of God and modeling to him or her what it looks like to live the Christian life. We are called to walk with people as they mature in their faith.

In the Great Commission the concept of making disciples involves both justification and sanctification. When justification occurs, the sinner is made right with God. They enter into a relationship with God. However, while this legal relationship with God is secure, we must also maintain and develop our fellowship with God on a daily basis through the process the Bible calls sanctification, which means "growth in holiness." The practice of knowing Him more and more deeply is how we become fully functional disciples. But we often forget that the goal is not intellectual knowledge but personal knowledge—fellowship. When we stop short at knowing God intellectually without knowing Him personally, it can lead to a legalistic mind-set that seems to focus only on Bible study and not outreach. When we focus only on gaining knowledge and not outreach, we fail to see that a key aspect of a disciple of Jesus is to be an incarnational missionary where God has placed us.

To better clarify this distinction, Bill Hull offers the following definitions:

- **Conversion:** "Theological slang" for when a person decides to become a Christian.
- **Discipleship:** Discipleship occurs when someone answers the call to learn from Jesus and others on how to live his or her life as though Jesus were living it.[2]

So according to the Great Commission, becoming a fully functioning disciple of Christ includes both justification and sanctification. Romans 3:23–24 says, "For all have sinned and fall short of the glory of God. They are justified freely by his grace through the redemption that is in Christ Jesus." That says we are saved and made righteous by the grace of Jesus who redeems us.

In 2 Timothy 2:2, Paul shows how God desires His children to grow and learn as they walk with Him. He says, "What you have heard from me in the presence of many witnesses, commit to faithful men who will be able to teach others also." The discipleship process was designed to be exponential and ongoing. Once people are saved, they should be mentored by other believers; and as they walk alongside mature disciples, they grow in their faith. As a part of their sanctification journey, they should also be trained to share their faith so that they too can do the work of ministry. As we've seen, part of being a disciple of Christ is understanding our call to be "seed scatterers" (Luke 8) and share our faith. And here is the way God designed it to work: When believers scatter enough seed, they will most likely lead someone to the Lord. At that point in this circular journey, they have the opportunity to walk with new believers in the same way others came alongside them when they first entered their relationship with the Lord.

Here's the problem: many churches don't have any sort of process for this. Not many churches are committed to walking with new believers or training them to replicate at all. In fact a recent study showed that only 52 percent of those who attended church in the last six months felt that their church was doing a good job of helping people grow spiritually.[3] Another statistic said that only two out of every ten Christians are engaged in some sort of discipleship activity.[4] And we wonder why so many of our churches seem void of fully functioning disciples who make more disciples.

Regaining Balance

About twice a year I make a commitment to start eating right and working out, and then for a few weeks or so, I'll frequent my local gym. Unaware of what I'm really supposed to do, I normally just start on one side of the building and begin working out. I lift the weights and use the machines in that area, and then, once I'm finished, I move on to the next area. In that part of the gym, I typically do the same thing. And then, once I've completed the machines in that area, I tend to move on to the other areas. As you can imagine, by the end of my workout, because of my ignorance, I will have used nearly every machine and lifted nearly every weight in the building. Then I go home, feel miserable, sit down on my couch, and convince myself that I should never go back again . . . but that's beside the point.

One thing I've noticed through my experiences in the gym. Not everyone works out the way I do. In fact, some guys never leave the barbell area. That's the part of the gym with a huge mirror on the wall, and in front of that mirror, there's a massive rack of weights ranging from ten pounds to more than one hundred pounds. The guys I'm referring to are *gym rats*, and they camp out in front of that mirror every day and put all of their effort and focus into building up their upper body. They'll do curls for hours. They'll build up their triceps and work diligently on their chest. After doing this day after day and week after week, as you can imagine, some of these guys have massive upper bodies.

But what's interesting about these gym rats is that if you look closely, most of these massive men have never worked out their legs. It truly is a common scene in front of the barbell mirror. Men lined up, and all of them with huge upper bodies and little bitty chicken legs.

Some of our churches look the same way. We appear to have skipped leg day too many times. It's easy for us to become disproportionate in our spiritual bodies when we focus too much on one thing or the other. However, even if we recognize this, we still have the option to move forward in a healthy way and regain balance in the seasons to come.

Regaining balance in evangelism and discipleship is often attempted in an overly reactive manner. If we are hurting in evangelism, we pump all our efforts into fixing that problem and end up ignoring discipleship as a result. Or, if we're hurting in discipleship, we put all our time and energy into evangelism to the detriment of discipleship. Thankfully, we do not have to choose between the two. This is so because, as mentioned above, you can't do one without the other. A church is not truly practicing evangelism unless its members are getting past their initial belief in the gospel and moving toward knowing Jesus personally. Furthermore, discipleship is not truly happening unless disciples are shown how to share their faith. Churches need to regain their balance!

In John 15:8, Jesus said, "My Father is glorified by this: that you produce much fruit and prove to be my disciples." In that verse alone, Jesus makes it plain as day: His disciples are going to replicate and make other disciples, and when we share our faith, lead others to Christ, and walk with them afterwards, Jesus says we *prove* (give evidence) that we are His disciples.

Larry Osborne, in his book *Mission Creep*, provides five recent shifts that describe how the church's work in evangelism and discipleship has been sabotaged and, therefore, has become imbalanced:

- A shift from *disciples* to *decisions*
- A shift from *obedience* to *doctrine*
- A shift from *persuasion* to *warfare*
- A shift from *people* to *numbers*
- A shift from *Jesus* to *justice*[5]

This imbalance creates a church that cannot and does not fulfill the Great Commission. The Great Commission involves the components of reaching *and* teaching people. This is only possible when the church is bearing fruit in the way Jesus described.

A disciple bears fruit. For this discussion we are talking about fruit that produces an evangelistic heart that desires to make disciples who make more disciples. When true disciples of Christ bear fruit, they focus on both evangelism and discipleship. There will be no separation.

Thankfully, we can regain the balance of evangelism and discipleship. In his book *Rediscovering Discipleship*, Robby Gallaty explained this concept perfectly. He said, "Evangelism and discipleship are two oars attached to the same boat. With only one oar in the water, you will row in a circle. Both oars are required to navigate in a straight line to reach your destination. We need evangelism and we need discipleship to carry out the Great Commission. The gospel is received through evangelism and then lived out through ongoing discipleship."[6]

Imbalance happens when we row with only one oar. Most churches tend to be either primarily *inward focused* or *outward focused*. Obviously, that would result from our natural leanings in the area of evangelism or discipleship. If you're naturally passionate and gifted in the area of discipleship, then most likely your focus is on growing up the people God has entrusted to you. If you're naturally passionate and gifted in the area of evangelism, then you're not primarily focused on the people you have because you're busy focusing on the people who aren't there yet. If we're going to function properly as the church and be balanced in our ministries, our focus has to be balanced.

When I served in Jackson, Tennessee, as the pastor of Englewood Baptist Church, our college ministry went through a season of rapid growth. Our new college pastor was doing a great job of being on campus and connecting with different groups in our community, and God really blessed this ministry in an incredible way. I'll never forget his coming into my office one day—he was so fired up! He told me of the hundreds of college students that were coming on Wednesday nights, and then he told me what he wanted to do next. He said, "I want to take the students who come for our large group, and out of those people, I want to create small groups." Of course my response was, "Great! That's awesome! Go for it!" But then he told me what he planned on calling these groups. He said, "Pastor, I've got a great name for our small groups. Ready? We're going to call them huddles." Then he concluded with, "Don't you love it?" I paused for a second. I'm sure the silence seemed awkward because I didn't respond right away, but when I did, my response was very simple. My response was, "I don't love it."

After the initial shock of my reaction, he stuck around to hear my explanation. I expounded: In the context of the church and what I believe God calls the church to be, I hate the word *huddle*. That simple word has a massive connotation that gives a picture of a small group of people that are 100 percent inwardly focused. In fact, while playing sports, I had been in several huddles throughout the years, so I could attest firsthand that when you are in a huddle, you are doing everything you can to prevent those on the outside from seeing or experiencing what is happening on the inside. In a huddle you get as tight as you can because you want to be able to discuss and plan and communicate with *your* group of people without anyone else peeking in. When you huddle up with your buddies, you are working as hard as you can to prevent anyone else from entering in. Quite simply, I hate the word *huddle* because God does not call us as the church to huddle up!

Unfortunately, many of our churches that live with the "discipleship church" stigma have received that tag because of huddles. Is anything wrong with sitting in circles and sipping coffee and debating theology and gaining more and more knowledge? There's not. In fact, nothing in that lineup is bad whatsoever; it's even good to huddle on occasion. But huddling up as the church becomes negative when huddling up is all we do. Many churches are imbalanced because they are stuck in the huddle, and they've forgotten that God has them on the field to run the next play and ultimately to win the game. It is possible, if your understanding of discipleship is incomplete, to "disciple" a church to death. What happens to a family that never leaves the house, never has any babies, and never adds any family members? Eventually that family dies off. We see that same scenario playing out in churches across our country. Believers cannot stay in our huddles.

Again, huddles in church don't have to be bad. In fact, the concept is designed to make the team more effective. The huddle was never designed to be the end result; running the next play is the goal! Scoring is the goal! Winning is the goal!

We huddle so we can strategize and learn and develop and be better prepared and equipped. We huddle so we can prepare for the next play. Once the church realizes how to maximize the huddle and get the team back on the field, it will experience the balance it's supposed to have.

Many churches are dying because they're primarily inward focused, but other churches are experiencing major imbalance issues because they are primarily outward focused. These churches train their people in one evangelism method on Thursday, another one on Friday, and then hit the streets Saturday through Wednesday knocking on doors. Their focus is primarily on the unchurched, the dechurched, and the prechurched—not the churched.

If we're going to be effective disciples of Christ, or effective in making disciples of Christ, we have to maintain a balance between shepherding the church on the inside and equipping the church to share on the outside. When we fail to maintain that balance, our churches will suffer from malnutrition.

The United Nations reports that more than 7.6 million people die annually throughout the world because of hunger-related causes. This means about 21,000 people, on average, die every day because of malnutrition or food insecurity. That's one person every 4 seconds![7] It makes you wonder how many of our churches are dying for similar reasons? How many of our people are sitting in the pews each Sunday, suffering and starving because what they're being fed is so one-sided and imbalanced?

After listening to questions like that, our tendency is to get defensive. We naturally want to defend our camps, and we say things like, "God made me to be an evangelist. It's my spiritual gift. He didn't create me with a desire to make disciples." Or we say, "God gifted me in the area of discipleship. I'm not extroverted. I don't have the gift of communication. I'm way better behind the scenes or in a small group setting." Just because you're good at one thing doesn't make you exempt from the other thing. Sticking to what we're good at or sticking to where we see results will eventually lead to imbalance.

Have you ever seen a marriage that's completely one-sided? It doesn't work. Earlier today I sat down with a couple who have been married for seven years. Next Wednesday their divorce will be finalized. The purpose of our meeting was simple; he doesn't want a divorce, but she does. As we sat in my office, he was pleading with his wife to reconsider. He was weeping and begging her to call off the divorce. He was making promise after promise. He was making commitment after commitment. But nothing he said even changed the expression on her expressionless face. For seven years their marriage had been completely one-sided, and now as they enter the final stretch of their marital relationship, it remains completely one-sided. Few things that involve multiple people and are one-sided work. We've got to be balanced, or we're going to be malnourished.

How to Prevent Discipling Your Church to Death

If we understand discipleship biblically, we know it includes evangelism and training for evangelism. But because many churches overemphasize discipleship at the expense of evangelism, they're at risk of discipling their church to death. How can we avoid doing this?

One answer to this complex question is this: maximize your huddle time *and* maximize your playing time. We've got to take full advantage of the time we have in huddles, but we've also got to commit to break out of our huddles more committed and more prepared to run the plays God calls us to run. That means we use our time with other believers to prepare to live on mission in the real world. It means we pray together and ask the Lord for boldness (Acts 4:23–31), and we sharpen one another (Prov. 27:17) so that we are better prepared to minister to those around us.

Some of us are way more comfortable doing life with the same people, and we don't necessarily like the idea of inviting new people into our church. For the church, that leads to a huge problem. As we mentioned earlier—if you never reproduce or invite new people into your family, eventually your family is going to cease to exist. God designed the church to replicate and reproduce, and when we neglect that truth, the aftereffect will be grim.

What are some indicators that we're too inward focused? When the calendar is overloaded with Bible studies and activities for our intellect with no room for hands-on ministry and evangelism, we have a problem. If the imbalance leans toward inward-focused discipleship, then the church will most likely be knowledgeable. However, it's possible to be knowledgeable and also malnourished. Discipleship does not exist for itself. If it does not lead us toward reaching others for Christ, then it's not real discipleship, and the church is in danger of becoming nothing more than another academic classroom.

James 1:22 says, "Be doers of the word and not hearers only, deceiving yourselves." James warns us in this passage to avoid thinking that just because we hear and believe a truth, we are living it out. Many Christians may understand the importance of evangelism in their minds and probably even enjoy hearing about the positive results of evangelism but are not personally taking advantage of God-given opportunities to express their faith. As James says, God's Word is not merely for hearing; it is primarily for doing.

Followers of Christ can easily deceive themselves, thinking that because they are part of a growing church, they have an evangelistic heart. Christ followers must walk in obedience in fulfilling the Great Commission according to the gifts God has given them. If not, they risk becoming spiritually obese because they are not working out (living) what they are digesting in God's Word. First Timothy 4:16 says, "Pay close attention to your life and your teaching; persevere in these things, for in doing this you will save both yourself and your hearers." This is telling us that we have to be intentional if we're going to maintain a healthy balance. When we as followers of Christ only focus on being hearers of God's Word, we will eventually become spiritually obese. The key to being spiritually fit is turning the caloric intake of God's Word into energy and activity by doing God's Word. In doing so, the believer will work off the meat of God's Word and transition to living the Word out daily.

Jesus didn't die in order to make us smarter sinners. The purpose of His death was to give hope to hopeless people who would in turn share that hope with more hopeless people. In a recent interview, Michelle Sanchez put it this way: "Discipleship ends in evangelism, and evangelism ends in discipleship."[8] It's two sides to the same coin. David Mathis said, "Let's be honest, disciple-making isn't rocket science. The vision is simple enough. Our need isn't for more information but to do what we already know we should do, and in some ways want to do, but simply haven't or aren't yet. Most of us know enough; we're just not doing it."[9]

CHAPTER 4

Do Your Job!

WHOSE RESPONSIBILITY IS it to fulfill the Great Commission?

In the Western church the clergy-laity divide has professionalized the Great Commission. Many people outsource a lot of tasks to other people (i.e., lawn care, car maintenance, childcare), and Christians have continued this trend with the task of evangelism. However, Jesus' words in the New Testament explicitly describe the evangelism task as not only for the clergy but for everyone. So clergy and laity can work together, we need to redefine the responsibilities of the evangelism task. Matthew 9:37–38 says, "Then he said to his disciples, 'The harvest is abundant, but the workers are few. Therefore, pray to the Lord of the harvest to send out workers into his harvest.'"

Jesus' words in this passage imply a sense of both *urgency* and *opportunity* when it comes to evangelism.[1] In an agricultural context the harvest time only lasts for a season. Thus, the farmer must take full advantage of the season. He must seize the opportunity while it is still present. Likewise, we must look at evangelism as something we must seize while the opportunity is present because it will not last forever.

Notice that Jesus said these words to His disciples. He told them to pray to the Lord and request that He send out people to reap the spiritual harvest that God had sown. He had used the disciples to sow the seeds, and now others were needed to do further work. As we clarify the responsibility of the Great Commission, we must realize that God, leaders, and laypeople all have various roles.

For a while, *College Gameday* on fall Saturday mornings had a segment of the show called, "You Had One Job!" In this segment sportscasters poked fun at unbelievable, simplistic errors people committed as a part of their role as a football player. Many of the videos shown were hilarious but also made an important point. No matter how many things we excel at, if we mess up at our primary job, we look like fools. The church's primary role is the Great Commission. This is our "one job." Doing well at other good things won't cut it if we ignore the primary thing God wants His church to succeed at—evangelism.

Ed Stetzer said, "Christians . . . seem to love evangelism, as long as someone else is doing it."[2] God has given His children a variety of gifts and opportunities, but He's given them to us with the same expectations and with the same task in mind. When we avoid obedience in this area, it's as if God were saying, "You had one job!"

Evangelism Is Your Responsibility

We are all co-laborers in the Great Commission. The thing that makes the Great Commission great are those two simple letters in the prefix—*co*.

If Jesus wanted to save the world all by Himself, He could have done it in a millisecond, but He chose to include us in His redemption plan for mankind. He enlisted us as coheirs with Christ. Romans 8:16–17 says, "The Spirit himself testifies together with our spirit that we are God's children, and if children, also heirs—heirs of God and coheirs with Christ—if indeed we suffer with him so that we may also be glorified with him." As coheirs, we've been enlisted to cooperate with God on this Great Commission.

Every follower of Christ needs to own the Great Commission. They cannot outsource it and depend on others to complete it. It is not only the pastor's job to evangelize. In fact, laypeople often have greater influence with their friends and peers than any pastor can. Every one of us has both the privilege and the responsibility of obeying the Great Commission, but many of us leave that responsibility to our paid church staff and other leaders. A dying world will never be won to Christ if only our church staff members are doing the work.[3]

God has given us each a gift, tools, and opportunities to play a role in this great task. It will take all of Christ's followers working together in an urgent manner in order to fulfill the Great Commission in this lifetime.

In Luke 12:8–9, Jesus says, "And I say to you, anyone who acknowledges me before others, the Son of Man will also acknowledge him before the angels of God, but whoever denies me before others will be denied before the angels of God."

> A dying world will never be won to Christ if only our church staff members are doing the work.

There are many reasons why we fail to evangelize. Chuck Lawless mentions several:

- Ignorance of what evangelism is.
- Few evangelistic role models.
- People aren't convinced about the lostness of unbelievers.
- No evangelism training is provided.
- Fear of the unknown.
- We have lost the joy of our own salvation.

- We don't know many unbelievers.
- We simply do not care.[4]

Each of these reasons must be overcome individually and from various angles because we have a responsibility to witness. Luke 12:8 makes clear that our responsibility before God is to represent Jesus to this lost world. I recently read a statistic that says over a fifteen-year period (1991–2005), 40 percent of American adults claimed to be born again. In 2017, only 31 percent made this same claim.[5] We don't have time to waste! As the world quickly becomes even more lost, the church must quickly become even more evangelistic.

"But I can't share my faith," you say. "I'm not gifted in the area of evangelism." "I don't know what it's like to lead someone to Jesus and disciple them." "I'm scared!"

There are so many reasons we don't tell people about Jesus, but not a single excuse is acceptable to God. Do you know why? It's because evangelism and discipleship are both 100-percent powered by God.

You say, "I can't do this well." That's okay, because you're doing it in the first place. For that simple reason God should get 100 percent of the credit for 100 percent of your ministry because He provides 100 percent of the power that leads to 100 percent of the results. In 1 Corinthians 3:6–7 Paul said, "I planted, Apollos watered, but God gave the growth. So then neither the one who plants nor the one who waters is anything, but only God who gives the growth." Do you know what that means in regards to evangelism? It means your job is to be obedient to share and nothing more. God never gave you a conversion quota. He never required you to close the deal. All God did was commission you to be obedient in sharing your faith and then to leave the results to Him. He's the one that gives the growth, and He's the only one capable of saving anyone.

It's hard to explain why we're so scared to share because we live in a world where sharing seems to be all we do. We share so much on social media—the awards our kids receive, the opportunities we get that we are "honored" to receive, the "blessings" we have, and not to mention, cat videos. Can you imagine if we spoke with one another one-on-one the same way we communicate via social media? We would drive each other crazy! We share so much on a daily basis, but we tend to avoid sharing the best news of all.

Social media has changed the world, and contrary to popular belief, it's no longer a millennial thing or a kid thing. According to Pew Research, 68 percent of all adults in America are now on Facebook, and 76 percent of these people say they check their Facebook at least once a day. After studying these numbers, social scientists have come to the conclusion that 56 percent of social media users are *addicted* to social media; and they attribute it to something called FOMO, which stands for "fear of missing out." It's an anxiety caused by the idea that something interesting is happening somewhere else and I don't want to miss out on it.[6]

We live in a world where people don't want to miss out. We don't want to miss anything—especially a great opportunity. Have you ever missed out on a great opportunity?

On May 10, 1976, Alexander Sinclair and RSO Records sent a letter to four teenage boys that went by the names, Bono, The Edge, Larry Mullen Jr., and Adam Clayton. The letter read, "Thank you for submitting your tape of 'U2' to RSO. We have listened with careful consideration, but feel it is not suitable for us to present. We wish you luck with your future career. Yours sincerely, Alexander Sinclair." Since the day they received that letter, U2 has gone on to record thirteen studio albums, win twenty-two Grammy Awards, and sell more than 170 million records worldwide.[7] They've become one of the world's best-selling musical artists of all time, and RSO records missed the opportunity to sign them while they were just kids looking for a break.

H. Jackson Brown once said, "In twenty years, you will be more disappointed by what you didn't do than by what you did."[8] That's certainly true for Alexander Sinclair; is it true for you?

Learning from Peter's Regrets

In the early days of the early church, Peter and John found themselves in a similar state, facing an inordinate,

God-sized opportunity. Peter and John were special disciples of Jesus. They were in His inner circle and, along with James, were the only disciples who witnessed Jesus' transfiguration (Matt. 17:1). Mark 14:33 tells us these men were also the only disciples with Jesus at Gethsemane so they really did have a backstage pass to Jesus' life on planet Earth.

Now, fast-forward to the days of the early church in Acts 3. Jesus had ascended, and the Holy Spirit had come to the disciples. Peter and John were the tip of the spear for bringing the gospel to the world. They were courageous evangelists. They were bold in their witness. But that hadn't always been the case.

Consider the backstory for this man named Simon. Simon was born around the year AD 1 and grew up on the Sea of Galilee in Israel. He was born and raised in a fishing village called Bethsaida, but around the year AD 25, he married a girl and moved into her mother's house on the other side of the sea in a small town called Capernaum. Historians describe Simon as a tall, slender man with a pale complexion. They say he had a short, thick, curly beard and had either thin eyebrows or no eyebrows at all.

By profession Simon was a fisherman. His father, Jonah (also known as John), and his brother, Andrew, were also fishermen, and together they had a partner in their business—a man named Zebedee, who had two sons named James and John. Now, Simon's brother Andrew was a disciple of John the

Baptist, and he was with John the Baptist in John 1 when Jesus walked by. In that moment, John 1:36 says, "When he saw Jesus passing by, he said, 'Look, the Lamb of God!'" In that moment Andrew believed Jesus to be the Messiah. After that happened, verses 41–42 says, "He first found his own brother Simon and told him, 'We have found the Messiah' (which is translated 'the Christ'), and he brought Simon to Jesus." Verse 42 goes on to say, "When Jesus saw him, he said, 'You are Simon, son of John. You will be called Cephas' (which is translated 'Peter')." So Jesus meets Simon and changes his name to Peter—which comes from the Greek word, *Petros*, meaning "rock."

Not long ago I was standing on the beach on the Sea of Galilee in the spot where Peter would have docked his fishing boat. It was also in that very spot where Jesus confronted them just days after Peter received his new name. That conversation is recorded in Matthew 4:18–20: "As he was walking along the Sea of Galilee, he saw two brothers, Simon (who is called Peter), and his brother Andrew. They were casting a net into the sea—for they were fishermen. 'Follow me,' he told them, 'and I will make you fish for people.' Immediately they left their nets and followed him."

When Jesus called Peter to follow Him, he didn't hesitate. And that's pretty impressive because he was a small business owner with responsibilities and obligations. He was married. He was busy. But in that setting the Messiah appeared to him and said, "Follow me." And he did! Peter didn't hesitate.

Peter went on to become a part of Jesus' inner circle and witnessed some incredible things while following Him. He witnessed miracles. He witnessed the transfiguration. He was called out by Jesus to walk on the water in Matthew 14.

If that wasn't enough, Peter was the one who was standing before the Lord in the pagan city of Caesarea Philippi when Jesus asked the question in Matthew 16:15, "Who do you say that I am?" And Peter responded in verse 16, "You are the Messiah, the Son of the living God."

Do you remember what happened next? Do you remember what Jesus said to Peter? "And I also say to you that you are Peter, and on this rock I will build my church, and the gates of Hades will not overpower it" (v. 18). Peter was a new man. His name had changed. His path had changed. His priorities had changed. He was following Jesus. He was a loyal, faithful, zealous, and courageous disciple of Christ.

Now fast-forward to the night of the crucifixion. The disciples had just eaten the Last Supper and were walking to the Mount of Olives to pray. As they were walking, Jesus looked at Peter and said, "Peter, you're going to deny me three times before a rooster crows." Peter replied to Jesus in Matthew 26:35, "Even if I have to die with you, . . . I will never deny you."

About that time they arrived at the garden of Gethsemane on the Mount of Olives. This was a beautiful, serene mountainside covered with shady olive trees, overlooking the panoramic landscape of the city of Jerusalem. Jesus was praying and agonizing because He knew what was about to happen. He told the disciples to pray, but the Bible says they couldn't stay awake. They finally woke up just in time to see Judas escorting a large crowd of people armed with swords and clubs to arrest Jesus.

Then Peter rose up and came to Christ's defense. He took out his sword and cut the ear off of one of the guards; then he had to stand there and watch as Jesus put the ear back on the man's head and healed the man. Jesus was then taken away to Caiphas's house (the high priest) where they would torture Him and hold Him prior to the crucifixion. Luke tells us that Peter followed them there.

So there Peter sat—in the courtyard at Caiphas's house—warming himself next to a firepit. And as he sat there, the Bible says he:

- Denied being with Jesus (Luke 22:57) when a servant girl approached him.
- Denied following Jesus (Luke 22:58) when someone else accused him.
- Denied knowing Jesus (Luke 22:60) when someone else insisted he was with Jesus.

Then at 3:00 a.m., Luke tells us, the rooster crowed. In that moment, verse 61 says, "The Lord turned and looked at Peter." And when He did, verse 62 says, "He went outside and wept bitterly."

In that moment Peter was rebellious. He rebelled against Jesus. He turned his back on Jesus. Out of convenience he rejected Him. Out of fear he denied Him. What Jesus said would happen, happened.

But let me show you something. Judas did the same thing, and yet his rebellion led to his destruction. In Matthew 27:4, Judas said, "I have sinned by betraying innocent blood." And verse 5 says, "He threw the silver into the temple and departed. Then he went and hanged himself."

You ask, "What's the difference in these two stories?" Why was Peter restored and not Judas? Because Judas never moved past his rebellion, but Peter's story didn't end there.

Peter's life had multiple stages.

1. Stage of Rebellion—In this stage Peter denied Christ and found himself living in disobedience to the commands of Christ.

2. Stage of Repentance—In this stage Peter turned away from his disobedience and pursued the will of God once again. Luke 22:62 says, "And he went outside and wept bitterly." In this passage Peter's heart was broken. He saw his rebellion against Jesus the same way God saw his rebellion.

As the story played out, Jesus was indeed crucified, and His body was placed in the tomb. Three days later Mary

Magdalene came running to tell Peter that Jesus' body wasn't in the tomb anymore, so Peter went to check it out, and sure enough, it was gone. We know that Jesus appeared ten times to many different people during those next forty days. However, take note of what Luke 24 tells us. It shows that Jesus appeared to Peter before the rest of the apostles.

John 21 tells us that Peter was fishing again when Jesus appeared. He had been fishing all day and all night and hadn't caught any fish, when suddenly a man yelled out from the shore (which was about a hundred yards away), saying (John 21:6), "'Cast the net on the right side of the boat.' . . . So they did, and they were unable to haul it in because of the large number of fish."

They caught 153 fish in one cast of the net, and Peter then realized that the man calling out to him was Jesus! So what did he do? In typical Peter style, he jumped in the water and swam to Jesus on the shore. Here's the cool part: while those guys were tending to the fish in the net, Jesus stayed on the beach. As He remained on that shore, Jesus did two things: He built a fire, and He cooked breakfast for His disciples.

> When they had eaten breakfast, Jesus asked Simon Peter, "Simon, son of John, do you love me more than these?"
>
> "Yes, Lord," he said to him, "you know that I love you."

"Feed my lambs," he told him. A second time he asked him, "Simon, son of John, do you love me?"

"Yes, Lord," he said to him, "you know that I love you."

"Shepherd my sheep," he told him.

(vv. 15–16)

For a long time I didn't understand why it *hurt* Peter when Jesus asked him the third time, but I get it now. The first two times Jesus asked him "Do you love me?," he used the verb *agape* in defining love. In other words, he was asking, "Do you love me with a complete love—an unconditional love?" And each time Peter answered, "You know I love you," but he used the word *phileo* (meaning: I love you like a *brother* or *friend*) instead of the word *agape*.

Now, the third time Jesus asked him was different. Jesus came down to Peter's word and asked him the question, "Do you love me?"—only this time He also used the word *phileo*. In other words, Jesus asked Peter, "Do you even love me as a friend?," and the text says it hurt Peter to hear those words.

Let me tell you why I think Peter didn't use the word *agape* at first. It's because at that point in his life, Peter was broken. He felt unworthy. He was aware of his disobedience. He felt convicted of his sin and had a sorrowful heart because of his rebellion. But what I want you to see is that after his rebellion and as a result of his repentance, the third stage Peter experienced was a stage of *restoration*. Jesus restored him and said, "Peter, feed my sheep! Get to work!" Peter was restored and equipped for God to use him!

Now let's look in the mirror. Peter's story can be our story as well. Perhaps you can relate to the guilt and shame Peter experienced after denying Christ. Maybe you've felt a conviction similar to what he would have felt in the courtyard that day. Here's the good news—the God who restored and used Peter is the same God who can restore us and use us. The God who took a coward and transformed him into one of the world's greatest evangelists can transform us into the faithful warriors he desires us to be.

As we move forward in this story, remember who Peter used to be and realize who God desires us to be. We will continue in Acts 3, but before we get there, remember where in the time line this story takes place.

- Day of Pentecost—The Holy Spirit fell on the early church: three thousand people were saved.
- Post-Pentecost—Peter and John were headed to the temple courts to pray.
- They met a beggar sitting by the Beautiful Gate who had been crippled his entire life. He asked them for money, and Peter responded, "I don't have gold or silver, but I'll give you something better than that:

get up and walk!" The Bible says the man stood to his feet and was instantly healed. The man started dancing and jumping, showing off his new ability to walk and giving praise to God. He went into the temple with Peter and John, and now the Jewish worshippers were beginning to notice what had happened.

Now Peter and John are with this beggar, a man everyone knew, and the crowds were coming. They wanted answers. Acts 3:11 says, "While he was holding on to Peter and John, all the people, utterly astonished, ran toward them in what is called Solomon's Colonnade." For Peter and John this had to be an intimidating scene. Remember, this was the first post-Pentecost miracle. This was all brand-new to them. And now, the Bible says, people were *running* at them.

Don't forget the time line here. Less than two months previous to this moment, Peter denied even knowing Jesus when a little girl approached him as he sat next to a firepit outside of Caiphas's house, and now a mob of people are running at him, trying to find out what just happened! For a split second you know he had to be thinking, *What am I going to say? What am I going to do?* But in that moment Peter realized that the Holy Spirit gives us boldness and courage.

Are you living with boldness today? Are you living your life as a courageous Christian? These characteristics come from walking in the Spirit.

I can just imagine Peter facing that moment with the words of Joshua 1:9 ringing in his ears. "Haven't I commanded you: be strong and courageous? Do not be afraid or discouraged, for the LORD your God is with you wherever you go." That alone ought to give us courage today! Remember this: Holy Spirit boldness comes from Holy Spirit fullness.

> Are you living with boldness today? Are you living your life as a courageous Christian? These characteristics come from walking in the Spirit.

That was true for Peter and John. The Holy Spirit was with them that day and gave them the courage to move forward and capitalize on the opportunity instead of being afraid and missing out on the opportunity. And it's true for us. The Holy Spirit replaces our *fear* with *faith*. That doesn't mean we will never be scared; it means when our natural tendency is to be scared, we can still move forward in faithful obedience. "When Peter saw this, he addressed the people: 'Fellow Israelites, why are you amazed at this? Why do you stare at us, as though we had made him walk by our own power or godliness? The God of Abraham,

Isaac, and Jacob, the God of our ancestors, has glorified his servant Jesus" (Acts 3:12–13).

When the Holy Spirit is working and moving, He never points to a human being. In fact, He never even points to Himself. Notice, when the Holy Spirit is working, He *always* points to Jesus.

In this moment, there was a large Jewish audience gathered around Peter, John, and the formerly lame beggar, and Peter seized the opportunity to say, "This man wasn't healed by our *power*—he was healed by our *God*!" It would have been real easy for these guys to stay silent and accept the praise they were about to be given, but their silence would have stolen the glory from God, so Peter spoke up and he set the record straight. The Holy Spirit replaces our inclination to stay silent with a determination to tell the truth. Most of the time when it comes to evangelism, our fear is what leads to our silence.

A few months ago I was flying across the country and ended up with a three-hour layover in the DFW airport. I found a comfortable table in the Admirals Club and decided to make the most of it with an orange juice and a big bowl of oatmeal. As I sat there enjoying my breakfast alone, I glanced up and noticed another guy at the table next to me sitting by himself as well. Something about this guy was familiar. I knew him from somewhere, but I couldn't put my finger on who he was. Then all of a sudden it clicked.

The guy sitting at the table next to me was none other than O. J. Simpson! I couldn't believe it. Seriously, I couldn't figure out how he could be sitting there because I had just watched the O. J. documentary on ESPN, and I thought he was still in jail. Apparently I was wrong! He was out, and now he was sitting right next to me.

So, what did I do? I pulled out my iPhone and slowly raised it to take a picture. I took several. After I took the photos, I quickly reviewed them on my screen, and I noticed on the last photo, O. J. was looking at the camera. I slowly raised my eyes to look back in his direction, and as I did, he was looking right at me, smiling.

I didn't know what to do. I froze for a second, unable to come up with the proper words to say. Then I noticed he was reading *Fantasy Football Magazine*, so I decided to break the awkward silence: "How's your fantasy football team looking this year?" As soon as I said it, I regretted it. But to my surprise he went with it. "My team's going to be pretty good, I think." I followed that up with an even dumber question: "Are any of your running backs as good as that guy O. J. Simpson was back in the day?" *What was I thinking?* But you know what? He thought it was hilarious. In fact, in that moment he stood up and walked over to my table with a magazine in one hand and a mimosa in the other, and then he sat down.

At this point I was freaking out, and in all seriousness, as O. J. approached my table, it was almost as if the Lord was speaking directly to me saying, "Hey Jordan, I set this whole thing up because I want you to tell him about Me. That's what this moment is about. This isn't about anything else. *You have one job*, and it's to share your faith with O. J."

Can I be honest? When I heard the Lord saying that to me, my first response was, "Absolutely not! No way!" In my mind there was no way I was about to talk to O. J. Simpson about Jesus. That very thought scared me to death. If I did tell him about Jesus, how would he respond? Would he be angry? I surely didn't want to make O. J. mad! Remember, I had just watched the documentary! But as I froze in that moment of fear, the Lord continued to press into me and show me that this moment was a divine appointment.

We talked about fantasy football. We talked about his golf game and how he had been working hard on his short game. We talked about airplanes and restaurants. You know what I've discovered? It's easy to talk about things that don't matter, but the devil makes it hard to talk about the thing that matters most. I overcame my fear that day, by the power of the Holy Spirit, and I said, "O. J., the best day I've had in my life was the day I realized I was a sinner because that was the day I asked Jesus to save me, and I haven't been the same since." At that point I looked him in the eye and asked him, "Have you ever had that experience in your life?" He looked at me and said, "You know, I've known Jesus my whole life." Then he stood up and said, "I've got to go now, but let's take a picture first." We snapped a few pictures, and then he left.

I wish I could tell you that O. J. prayed to receive Christ that day, but that's not what happened. You know what did happen though? I overcame everything the devil threw at me, overcame my fear, and did what Jesus wanted me to do. That's our job. Our job isn't to save. Our job is to obey and to share and to trust God with the results.

> It's easy to talk about things that don't matter, but the devil makes it hard to talk about the thing that matters most.

Have you ever missed an opportunity to tell someone about Jesus? Have you ever blown it when you felt led to share the gospel? Has there been a time when you knew God wanted you to tell someone how to be saved, and yet you didn't speak up? Fear! The devil will use it to keep you silent. You say, "I just didn't feel like it would have made a difference. I don't think I could have been successful in sharing Jesus." What exactly does it mean to be successful in sharing Jesus? And how would you know anyway? God is the one who saves, not you! I once heard someone say, "Success in witnessing is simply taking the initiative to share Christ in the power of the Holy Spirit and leaving the results to God."[9] I like that.

When we share Jesus, we are successful 100 percent of the time. And you know what? The devil knows that. That's why he covers you in so much fear at the thought of sharing your faith. As one author noted, evangelism is really just a conversation, and normally *both* people are really nervous. But nobody ever said sharing Jesus would be easy. But when we are inclined to stay silent, the Holy Spirit can empower us with a determination to tell the truth. As nerve-racking as it must have been, in this moment, Peter preached the truth!

> The God of Abraham, Isaac, and Jacob, the God of our ancestors, has glorified his servant Jesus, whom you handed over and denied before Pilate, though he had decided to release him. You denied the Holy and Righteous One and asked to have a murderer released to you. You killed the source of life, whom God raised from the dead; we are witnesses of this. By faith in his name, his name has made this man strong, whom you see and know. So the faith that comes through Jesus has given him this perfect health in front of all of you. (Acts 3:13–16)

Peter wasn't going to miss out on this opportunity! But you've got to admit, it took some guts to say what he said to the crowd that day. He didn't tell them what they *wanted* to hear; he told them what they *needed* to hear. Think about it. If you were in that crowd, wouldn't you have wanted to hear the truth? If you were diagnosed with a disease, you wouldn't want your doctor to spare your feelings and lie to you. You would want your doctor to tell you the truth so that you could get better! The truth hurts sometimes; but just like a disease, you have to hear about your problem if you're going to address it. Nobody wants to hear, "You're a messed-up person. You're a sinner. You need help. You need to be saved." But it's the truth! And without hearing the truth and responding to the truth, the Bible says, we will die without the Lord and will spend eternity separated from Him in a real place called hell.

Do you believe that's the truth? Of course you do. But I guess the real question is, Do you love people enough to tell them the truth? Jesus said in John 13:34, "Love one another. Just as I have loved you, you are also to love one another." In Matthew 22:39, He said, "Love your neighbor as yourself." In Matthew 5:44, He said, "Love your enemies." His message was consistent. Jesus told us to love everyone. When we share Him with others, we obey this command and demonstrate that love. But when we stay silent, we disobey our Savior, and we are unfaithful to this commandment.

Peter and John carried with them the love of God! They were also filled with the Spirit of God. That Spirit replaced their inclination to stay silent with a determination to tell the truth.

In this passage Peter is preaching again, and notice, he's not preaching like the scared Peter who denied Christ. He's preaching with passion and fearlessness. Why? Because Peter had the Holy Spirit, and the Holy Spirit had replaced his fear with faith. In this passage he boldly proclaimed that Jesus was the Messiah, and now he's pointing fingers at the religious crowd, saying, "You killed him!" He didn't hold back. He didn't cower to the crowd. He said, "You disowned the holy and righteous One. . . . You killed the author of life. . . . You killed the Son of God."

Maybe you're wondering: *Why did he have to say that? Why did he kick this sermon off by reminding them of all the horrible things they had done?* And the answer is: Before people can be saved, they have to realize what they're being saved from. You can't be forgiven of your sin until you first recognize the fact that you are a sinner! You can't get to the good news until you've understood the bad news. That's what's happening here. Peter is preaching truth. He's telling them the truth. And the bad news of sin is *part* of the truth. But thanks be to God, the bad news of sin isn't the *whole* truth!

> And now, brothers and sisters, I know that you acted in ignorance, just as your leaders also did. In this way God fulfilled what he had predicted through all the prophets—that his Messiah would suffer. Therefore repent and turn back, so that your sins may be wiped

out, that seasons of refreshing may come from
the presence of the Lord, and that he may
send Jesus, who has been appointed for you as
the Messiah. Heaven must receive him until
the time of the restoration of all things, which
God spoke about through his holy prophets
from the beginning. Moses said: The Lord
your God will raise up for you a prophet like
me from among your brothers and sisters. You
must listen to everything he tells you. And
everyone who does not listen to that prophet
will be completely cut off from the people. In
addition, all the prophets who have spoken,
from Samuel and those after him, have also
foretold these days. (Acts 3:17–24)

Peter began this message to the people by pointing out the
bad news of sin. But in verse 17, he changes his tone and begins
to share with them the good news of grace. When you preach
the truth, it should include both of these things. He concedes
in verse 17 that the Jews may have "acted in ignorance" and
seems to compassionately provide them with an opportunity
to rethink their conclusions about who the Messiah would be.
In verses 19–20, Peter urges the Jewish audience to repent and
accept Jesus as the Messiah so that their sins would be forgiven
and they could experience new life in Christ. "Repent and

turn back, so that your sins may be wiped out, that seasons of refreshing may come from the presence of the Lord."

Peter looked at the crowd that day and reminded them, "You knew a prophet was coming—following the line of previous prophets—and you knew He would be the Messiah. You knew that!" Then he pointed them to the prophecy of Moses in Deuteronomy 18:15, and he connected that prophecy to Jesus. In other words, Peter stood before this huge crowd of Jews and boldly proclaimed and revealed that the Jesus they rejected and killed was indeed the Messiah they had longed for. "You are the sons of the prophets and of the covenant that God made with your ancestors, saying to Abraham, And all the families of the earth will be blessed through your offspring. God raised up his servant and sent him first to you to bless you by turning each of you from your evil ways" (vv. 25–26).

He said to them in verse 25, "You are physical descendants— you are a part of the lineage." In this text he's quoting Genesis 12:3, "I will bless those who bless you, I will curse anyone who treats you with contempt, and all peoples on earth will be blessed through you."

Peter then went on to say God's purpose was for them to be used by God to tell people to repent and believe in Jesus. God wanted to bless Israel first, and then He would bless the world through Israel. He said, "You are *connected* to Jesus. You are *called* by Jesus. And today you can *repent* and *be saved* by

Jesus." As Peter preached, notice that he directed all the attention to Jesus.

- God's Son and Servant (v. 13)
- The Holy and Righteous One (v. 14)
- The Author of life (v. 15)
- The name of Jesus (v. 16)
- His Messiah (v. 18)
- The Lord (v. 19)
- The Messiah, Jesus (v. 20)
- The Prophet (vv. 22–23)
- The Offspring of Abraham (v. 25)
- God's Servant (v. 26)

This entire sermon is pointing people to Jesus. Peter is pleading with this religious Jewish crowd, "Repent and turn back, so that your sins may be wiped out, that seasons of refreshing may come from the presence of the Lord" (vv. 19–20). This wasn't a popular message in that day. Some people were upset and angry that Peter would make such a bold declaration in the temple court. But he didn't miss out on the opportunity that God put before him. God filled him. God empowered him, and God used him greatly. And through his obedience and faithfulness, Acts 4:4 tells us, *many* believed after hearing him speak, and more than five thousand men repented from their sin and were saved that day.

Nearly six hundred years before that happened, the prophet Ezekiel spoke these words:

> "Repent and turn from all your rebellious acts, so they will not become a sinful stumbling block to you. Throw off all the transgressions you have committed, and get yourselves a new heart and a new spirit. Why should you die, house of Israel? For I take no pleasure in anyone's death." This is the declaration of the Lord GOD. "So repent and live!" (Ezek. 18:30–32)

God honors our obedience in sharing the gospel. What was the result of Peter's boldness that day? What was the outcome of his obedience? Five thousand people who heard Peter preach this message of hope repented of their sins and believed Jesus for salvation. What will be the result when you share your faith?

The Pastor's Role in Leading an Evangelistic Church

IF THE SHEPHERD doesn't lead, the sheep will not follow.

Don't get me wrong. It is indeed everyone's responsibility to participate in evangelistic efforts. However, if the pastor isn't leading the charge, those he's shepherding will most likely never go to a place to which he hasn't led them. While equipping the saints for the service of evangelism, he is not only an equipper; he is also an example of how one should participate in evangelism. He should demonstrate his engagement in evangelism through his heart and practice. He should pray for the lost, live in a way that points people to Christ, and naturally share his faith in Christ as a part of his lifestyle.

First Peter 5:2–3 says, "Shepherd God's flock among you, not overseeing out of compulsion but willingly, as God would have you; not out of greed for money but eagerly; not lording it over those entrusted to you, but being examples to the flock."

The concluding phrase of this passage emphasizes the main point of the character traits before it. The pastor is to exercise oversight not because he has to or so that he can benefit. He is to lead out of his passion, willingly, with a servant's heart. Why is he to do this? Because he is an example to his church. Knowing that Peter wrote these words, one can easily imagine that Peter was probably talking also to himself.

Fortunately, pastors are not left without an example. They can look to Jesus just as Paul did. In 1 Corinthians 11:1, Paul said, "Imitate me, as I also imitate Christ." Joel Green states, "As Jesus is the Chief Shepherd and elders are shepherds, so Jesus provides the 'pattern' and elders a 'model.' Their leadership is realized in their embodiment of the character of Christ."[1] Jesus naturally shared the gospel both with his life and with his words. The pastor must know Jesus intimately if he is to be an example to his church in the practice of evangelism.

In this entire chapter we're preaching to the choir because those of us who are pastors already know that evangelism should be part of what we do and who we are. We know it. In fact, 97 percent of surveyed pastors say they believe it is their "responsibility" to model personal evangelism.[2] But even though we're keenly aware of our evangelistic responsibility, there are still many pastors telling people they should share but never embracing evangelism as part of their own lifestyle.

God's doesn't expect pastors to simply coach from the sidelines. He expects every pastor to be a player-coach. A player-coach is one who holds both the position of the coach of a team and a player on the team.

Famous baseball player-coaches include Tris Speaker, Jimmy Collins, and John McGraw. Basketball player-coaches include Bill Russell and Lenny Wilkens. Some would also include Lebron James into that lineup, but he hasn't officially made that jump quite yet. In many ways the pastor is not just a coach telling everyone else what to do; he is also a player on the evangelism team, modeling what it looks like to embrace a lifestyle of sharing Christ.

Everything rises and falls on leadership. Pastors cannot expect their staff, their deacons, their lay leaders, or their congregations to do something they aren't modeling and/or prioritizing.

I've had the privilege of serving under several well-respected pastors in some great churches, and one thing I've learned from serving in these roles is that over time the church begins to look like its pastor. That's been true in every church where I've served.

I served for several years on the staff of Prestonwood Baptist Church in Plano, Texas, under Pastor Jack Graham. Dr. Graham is an incredible leader. He is a man's man with a passion for evangelism and a desire to reach people, and he wants everything done at a high level of excellence. It didn't take us long to realize why Prestonwood was such a dynamic, booming church. They had a phenomenal men's ministry— one of the best in the country. They had the most pristine facilities of any church we'd ever seen. They were baptizing more than a thousand people a year. And everything—from the nursery to the workshop—was well thought out and first class. How did they get to that place? The answer is leadership. That church over time had taken on the personality and passions of its pastor.

During another season in my ministry, I had the privilege to serve at First Baptist Atlanta alongside "America's Pastor," Dr. Charles Stanley. This is another one of those seasons in ministry I'll cherish forever. To this day I've never heard a better Bible teacher than Dr. Stanley. For a couple of years, he poured into me and gave me opportunities to learn and grow as a communicator and a pastor, and for that I'll be eternally grateful.

Dr. Stanley was much different from Dr. Graham. He is passionate about Bible study. He is focused on teaching God's Word and getting those teachings to the *ends of the earth* through radio and television. He is passionate about southern gospel quartets and global missions.

Naturally, after nearly forty years of pastoring the people at First Baptist Atlanta, you can guess what this congregation is passionate about. They love southern gospel quartets. They love global missions. In fact, they host one of the nation's largest global missions conferences each year. They also love Dr. Stanley's Bible teaching and make a priority of listening to him teach each week.

If the pastor isn't a church-growth guy, there's a good chance his church isn't experiencing church growth. If the pastor isn't prioritizing and emphasizing evangelism or celebrating life change on a regular basis, there's a good chance that isn't happening either. We as pastors have a huge responsibility and an even greater opportunity to lead our people to prioritize what Jesus tells us to prioritize. But at the same time, the gospel should be our passion, not our business.

In her book *Unbinding the Gospel*, author Martha Reese reveals that in many mainline churches pastors do not engage in personal evangelism.[3] There are several reasons this could be the case. One writer provided the following tips for pastors to keep them focused on personal evangelism:

1. Talk about Christ with at least one person weekly.
2. Be visible.
3. Pray daily.
4. Expand your circle of influence.
5. Respond to cries for help.[4]

Do the Work of an Evangelist

Paul wrote to his mentee pastor Timothy in 2 Timothy 4:5: "But as for you, exercise self-control in everything, endure hardship, do the work of an evangelist, fulfill your ministry." Pastors today, like Timothy, need to remember that "the work of an evangelist" is part of the ministry of a Christian pastor.

It is very easy for the modern pastor to easily focus on the important duties of serving the church but forget to "do the work of an evangelist." There are so many distractions faced by pastors every day that they can forget about the Great Commission.

Several years ago the movie *Up* popularized the hunting dog's notion to easily be distracted from his primary purpose of what he is hunting. The movie used the distraction of a squirrel and had the particular hunting dog yell "Squirrel!" every time he saw a squirrel—right in the middle of doing something important. Pastors can also have "squirrels" in their daily lives that distract them from their primary purpose of evangelism and discipleship. We experience distractions at home, on social media, and even at church.

Sometimes we get so busy working on sermons, reading, studying, and parsing verbs in the original languages that we forget why we're doing it in the first place. Just think about all the things a pastor is responsible for each week: births, deaths, and everything in between. Marriage counseling. Teaching and equipping. Message prep. Deacons meetings. Committee meetings. Meetings with angry people. Meetings with happy people. Visiting the sick. Following up with the guests. Coaching his staff. And we haven't even mentioned praying.

Pastors are some of the busiest people in the world, and the devil has a way of using that busyness to prevent us from focusing on the main thing. We can't let the good distract us from the essential.

These ancillary duties often distract the pastor and turn him into little more than a figurehead who is respected in the community as a professional. However, he cannot ignore his responsibility to be salt and light in a dark world that is desperate for hope. For the pastor to maintain focus, he must create a habitual lifestyle where an evangelistic heart is his primary nature. Then he won't have to remember to do evangelism; it'll go from being something he does to the person he is. And when the pastor has become an evangelist, his church will begin emphasizing evangelism as well. The sheep will follow their shepherd.

I learned how to throw a baseball by watching my dad throw a baseball. I also learned how to shoot a basketball, ride a bike, tie my shoes, shave my face, and tie a tie the same way—by watching my dad model them. Come to think of it, that's how I learned how to share the gospel as well.

When I was a little boy, my dad was pastoring a little church in Springtown, Texas. Every week he and a handful of deacons met at the church for a time of prayer, and then they got in their cars and went all over town for something they called *visitation*. This is where people are equipped to share their faith, and defend their faith, and then they are mobilized to go all throughout the community to do so.

I don't know if it was because we couldn't afford a baby-sitter at the time or what, but for whatever reason my dad dragged me along to visitation on a consistent basis. I can't tell you how many living rooms I sat in—never saying a word, just sitting there like a fly on the wall—watching my dad's pattern of navigating the dialogue and fielding the questions and always, *always* leading the conversation back to Jesus.

I'm not sure if it was intentional, but as he exposed me to that environment and gave me a seat at the table while he modeled personal evangelism, he was training me in more ways than one. To this day he's never sat me down and walked me through a step-by-step training guide on how to share my faith; he didn't have to because I've had the opportunity to watch him model it my entire life.

Pastors do the same thing when they give an invitation at the end of the sermon. When a pastor walks his congregation through the process of repentance and faith and salvation, he is evangelizing the sinner, but he's also equipping the saint. The sheep follow what the shepherd models.

Titus 2:7–8 says, "Make yourself an example of good works with integrity and dignity in your teaching. Your message is to be sound beyond reproach, so that any opponent will be ashamed, because he doesn't have anything bad to say about us."

CHAPTER 5

Overcoming Obstacles That Prevent Health

EVERY SEPTEMBER ACROSS the state of Tennessee, thousands of enthusiastic challengers participate in "mud runs" and "obstacle races." The registration fee starts at fifty dollars for those who register early, and the participants can choose either the 5K (3.1 miles) or the 10K (6.2 miles) competition.

The 5K courses include twenty-plus military style obstacles, and the 10K consist of forty-plus similar obstacles that each runner must confront and conquer. Each obstacle on the course is designed to challenge each competitor physically and mentally. The greatest challenge is not so much the distance as it is the obstacles, which include gorilla ropes, the low crawl, the rope swing, the minefield, the leap of faith, the rope bridge, and tunnels, to name a few.

The crazy thing is, *people actually pay money to put themselves through it.* Their registration web page includes this note: "EMS (Emergency Medical Services) will be on sight." I certainly hope so!

If you have ever run a 5K or a 10K, you know running that distance can be challenging. But to include a variety of obstacles along the way drastically intensifies the challenge. It's like adding ten hurdles to a 400-meter race. The 400-meter race is challenging enough, but to add ten hurdles only increases the challenge. That's what obstacles do; they increase the challenge.

Because those who register for these races know going into it that they will have obstacles to overcome, they prepare for those obstacles. They physically train and mentally prepare months before the race not only to go the distance but also to overcome anything that might stand in their way.

As the race gets started and the competitors approach the first obstacle, nobody's caught off guard. Nobody thinks, *Who put that on the path? Where did that come from? I didn't anticipate that!* No, they all know going into the race that they will have obstacles to overcome in order to finish the race. Not one runner is surprised or caught off guard when facing various obstacles.

Evangelism is more like a mud run than a simple 5K or 10K. We don't just have to go the distance; we have to overcome obstacles along the why. But unlike people competing in these obstacles courses, most Christians are unprepared. We're often surprised by the obstacles we must confront and conquer! We're shocked at the things that hinder our progress as we hope to share the gospel.

The reality is, sometimes obstacles can be removed, but most often they must be overcome. No one ever said that it would be easy!

Obstacles to Evangelism

The dictionary defines *obstacle* as something "that opposes, stands in the way of, or holds up progress toward some goal."[1] Who or what currently stands in the way of your evangelistic efforts? What is slowing you down? If you were to create an obstacle list and write down every hindrance to your personal and church evangelistic efforts, what would make your list?

What if the apostle Paul had a personal obstacle list that indicated his greatest opposition to the gospel? What would make his list? Where would he start? The same place we should start!

Enemy Number One

The greatest obstacle Paul faced in his day is the same great obstacle we face today: the devil and his army. Here is how Paul described his greatest hindrance to the believers in Ephesus: "For our struggle is not against flesh and blood, but against the rulers, against the authorities, against the cosmic powers of this darkness, against evil, spiritual forces in the heavens. For this reason take up the full armor of God, so that you may be able to resist in the evil day, and having prepared everything, to take your stand" (Eph. 6:12–13).

The greatest obstacle we face when it comes to our evangelistic efforts is the one Jesus referred to in John 14:30 as "the ruler of the world," and Paul referred to as "the god of this age" (2 Cor. 4:4) and "the ruler of the power of the air" (Eph. 2:2).

The bottom line is that the devil's sole goal in life is to keep God from getting the worship God deserves. Therefore, he is out to stop any and every attempt to share the gospel. He is our greatest obstacle!

At the root of every obstacle that slows down sharing of the gospel message is Satan and his effort to deny God the glory God deserves. He can work through anyone (inside or outside the church) to discourage, derail, and sometimes even defeat our evangelistic efforts.

He not only provides obstacles; he *is* the obstacle! He works overtime to find ways to prevent gospel seeds from being sown. And where the gospel seed has been sown, he often finds ways to prevent it from germinating.

In the parable of the soils, Jesus tells us in Matthew 13:19, "When anyone hears the word about the kingdom and doesn't understand it, the evil one comes and snatches away what was sown in his heart."

Then later, in verses 38–39 in the parable of the tares, Jesus explains, "The field is the world; and the good seed—these are the children of the kingdom. The weeds are the children of the evil one, and the enemy who sowed them is the devil. The harvest is the end of the age, and the harvesters are angels."

Jesus describes our enemy not only as a snatcher of true seed but also as a sower of false seed. He is a snatcher and a sower! That's what our enemy does. Our enemy is always lurking in the shadows wherever the gospel is being shared, attempting to snatch it up quickly before it lands in a hungry heart, and he's always sowing false seeds along the way.

> Whenever we initiate a conversation with someone about Jesus, our adversary initiates an obstacle.

Here's what that means for us: whenever we initiate a conversation with someone about Jesus, our adversary initiates an obstacle. But be encouraged, "the one who is in you is greater than the one who is in the world" (1 John 4:4).

Are We Our Own Worst Enemy?

The reality today is that, most often, it is not our enemy snatching up the gospel seeds as much as our not sowing the gospel seed at all. Our enemy doesn't have much seed to snatch up!

"Study after study shows that most Christians have never shared their faith—most indicating that somewhere around

90 percent of evangelicals have never shared their faith with anyone outside of their family. (Kind of makes you wonder how we get away with using the name 'evangelical'!)."[2] In a recent LifeWay Research study, only 20 percent of churches in the United States are growing, and only 1 percent are growing by reaching lost people.[3]

One measurement the Southern Baptist Convention—the largest American Protestant denomination—uses to determine its evangelistic success is the number of church members it takes to produce one baptism. Keep in mind that these ratios are not exact because many SBC churches fail to report their annual baptism numbers. But for the sake of comparison, in 1940, the SBC was averaging about one baptism per twenty-five members.[4] For those reporting, in 2017, the ratio was one baptism per fifty-nine members,[5] with a total of 254,122 people being baptized, which was 26.5 percent fewer than in 2007!

Houston, we have a problem! If our churches do not discover soon how to overcome their obstacles for effectively doing evangelism, it will only be a matter of time until we become obsolete.

"The man who is good for excuses," said Benjamin Franklin, "is good for little else."[6] For many, making excuses is as common as taking a breath of air or going to sleep at night.[7] An excuse is something we give for not doing something we know we're supposed to do. It is time we stop rationalizing and making excuses for our lack of evangelism. Like the participants of the mud runs and obstacle races, it's time to face our obstacles and learn how to conquer them.

Every competitor in the mud runs and obstacle races must identify each obstacle, make an assessment, and then determine the best course of action to take in order to overcome it. Using that same technique, we need to begin by identifying what hinders us from sharing the gospel and then determine the best course(s) of action to take to overcome it.

Apathy: I Don't Care

Do you care that your neighbor is going to hell? Do you care that people you work with are going to hell? Do you care that you have family members who are going to hell?

I'm afraid that way too many of us have the *Jonah complex*, who didn't care if the Ninevites went to hell or not. In fact, the prophet Jonah knew they deserved hell and wanted to make sure they got it! You can know that he wasn't losing any sleep over the eternal destiny of the godless Ninevites.

Rather than having a passion in his heart to see the Ninevites come into a relationship with God, his heart was filled with apathy. If apathy for reaching the lost for Christ can happen to a prophet of God, it can happen to anybody!

His apathy soon turned into rebellion against God. His rebellion against God landed him inside a big fish for three days and three nights. By the way, God never blesses disobedience, only obedience!

After being vomited onto dry land, Jonah proceeded to deliver the message God gave him: "In forty days Nineveh will be demolished!" (Jonah 3:4). That was it! A seven-word sermon! The next verse says, "Then the people of Nineveh believed God. They proclaimed a fast and dressed in sackcloth—from the greatest of them to the least."

God took that heartless seven-word sermon delivered by His prophet, and the entire city came to God! And Jonah? We read in Jonah 4:1, "Jonah was greatly displeased and became furious." If that wasn't bad enough, we hear Jonah praying in chapter 4, "And now, LORD, take my life from me, for it is better for me to die than to live" (v. 3).

Back in the 1970s when I was in the student ministry of Lake Highlands Baptist Church in Dallas, Texas, we often sang a chorus written by Bill Cates that challenged us in regard to our apathy. The song was titled "Do You Really Care?," and the refrain went like this: "Do you really care? Do you know how to share with people everywhere? Do you really care? Will you take the dare? Spread good news everywhere? The cross of Christ to bear? Do you really care?"[8]

The words of that little chorus got into my teenage mind and heart and have remained there for a lifetime. The prophet Jonah didn't get it. He didn't care about the souls of those

Ninevites, even if it meant rebelling against God's direction in his life.

Apathy says, *I just don't care.* But you and I should be eternally grateful for those who cared enough about us to overcome the *apathy obstacle* and tell us about Jesus.

So, how do you overcome apathy? Overcoming the apathy obstacle begins with *prayer.* A good place to start is with the "I just don't care for the lost" prayer. Let's face it: apathy is an obstacle to our sharing Jesus, and He knows it. We are not fooling God! He knows if we don't care, and overcoming it begins by an honest confession to God.

How long should your "I just don't care for the lost" prayer last? Until God roots it out! It's the kind of praying Jesus was talking about in Matthew 7:7–8, "Ask, and it will be given to you. Seek, and you will find. Knock, and the door will be opened to you. For everyone who asks receives, and the one who seeks finds, and to the one who knocks, the door will be opened."

All three verbs used by Jesus (*ask, seek,* and *knock*) are present-tense verbs, which speak of continual action. "Ask and keep on asking. Seek and keep on seeking. Knock and keep on knocking."

The next step to overcoming the apathy obstacle is *power.* Paul tells us in Ephesians 5:18, "And don't get drunk with wine, which leads to reckless living, but be filled by the Spirit."

The apostle Paul wants us to be filled and keep on being filled with the Holy Spirit.

The power needed for overcoming the *apathy obstacle* is the Holy Spirit's power. He produces and provides the necessary power for overcoming apathy. Rather than grieving the Holy Spirit (Eph. 4:30) by having known sin in your life; rather than stifle the Holy Spirit (1 Thess. 5:19) by saying no when He says yes or by saying later when He says now, be filled with the Spirit and experience obstacle-bursting power.

Overcoming the apathy obstacle also involves *perception*. Start seeing people as Jesus sees people. We read in Matthew 9:36, "When he [Jesus] saw the crowds, he felt compassion for them, because they were distressed and dejected, like sheep without a shepherd."

British pastor Tim Chester says that evangelism is "doing normal life with gospel intentionality." As we go through our lives, we are aware that people all around us are in need of the gospel, and we look and pray for ways to share it with them.[9]

Start seeing people the way Jesus sees people: lost, hopeless, spiritually dead, separated from God, without peace. That's our business! The barber will not look at a person's shoes to see if they are shined. He will look at their hair: how it's cut, how long it is, what color it is. His focus is on a person's hair because that's his business.

Our focus must get on the condition of the souls of those we encounter each day, whether they are lost or saved. That is our business and must become our focus in order to overcome and move beyond the *apathy obstacle.*

Apprehension: I'm Too Afraid

There are several other obstacles that hinder our efforts in getting the gospel to the lost. One is the *apprehension obstacle* that says, *"I'm too afraid."*

There are four things that can happen when sharing Jesus: you meet a fellow believer, a seed is planted, someone comes to Christ, or someone rejects the message. It's usually that last one that scares us, which results in our not sharing Jesus.

First Peter 4:14 states, "If you are ridiculed for the name of Christ, you are blessed, because the Spirit of glory and of God rests upon you." It's not when we are rejected that we should fear, but when we are silent.[10]

Keep in mind that we are not responsible for the outcome of our witnessing. That's God's business. Our business is to take the initiative to share Jesus in the power of the Holy Spirit and leave the results to God.

> We are not responsible for the outcome of our witnessing. That's God's business.

Abdication: It's Not My Responsibility

The *abdication obstacle* says, *"It's not my responsibility."* It was normal in the New Testament for converts to tell their friends and family about Jesus.[11] Andrew told his brother Peter (John 1:41). Matthew brought many of his friends to meet Jesus (Mark 2:13–15). Cornelius brought his family and friends to Jesus (Acts 10:24, 44). Timothy was introduced to Jesus by his mother and grandmother (2 Tim. 1:5).

Sharing Jesus was the normal Christian experience and practice in the New Testament era. Yet many of us have abdicated the responsibility of personal evangelism as though it was simply not our job.

Mark Dever, in his book *Nine Marks of a Healthy Church*, says, "I'm convinced that one of the distinguishing marks of a healthy church is a biblical understanding and practice of evangelism."[12] In other words, sharing Jesus is the responsibility of every believer, and it is a sign of a thriving, obedient congregation.

Inadequacy: I Don't Know Enough

The *inadequacy obstacle* says, "I don't know enough. It's better if I just leave evangelism to the professionals." That's not the New Testament pattern for sharing Jesus. Those who permit the *inadequacy obstacle* to hinder them from sharing Jesus often say, "Shouldn't it be done by those who really know how to do it? I mean, it is so often done badly. I wouldn't want to add to that! I don't know enough."[13]

Charles Kelley, in his book *Fuel the Fire,* reminds us that when a driver loses control and the car filled with his family runs off the road and into a lake, it's not just the passing firemen or policemen who should stop. They may have superior training and ability in rescue techniques, but the rancher with a rope and the teacher who can swim must help if they are the first ones on the scene. A saving relationship with Jesus is qualification enough for any person to tell another how to be born again. More than that, it is a qualification that requires a person to be a witness.[14]

To you who are members of a Bible-believing church that have been overcome by the *inadequacy obstacle,* let me say as kindly as I know how: you cannot pay your pastor and staff to do your evangelism. Yes, the pastor and staff are to be actively sharing Jesus, but they cannot do the amount of sharing necessary to shake a community for Christ! Go back and read through the book of Acts, and you will discover that sharing Jesus was part of the normal Christian life! I read years ago that when it comes to evangelism *we have become so abnormal that we've become normal and to become normal would make us abnormal.*

To those who have not conquered the inadequacy obstacle: ask for help! To those who have overcome it: start helping those who haven't! Pastors, I plead with you to begin training your members to share Jesus!

Ever believer is a participant in the obstacle race called life. Time is short. People are lost. People need Jesus. Once the *apathy obstacle* is confronted and conquered, all other obstacles can be overcome. Once you start caring for people and seeing them as Jesus does, your compassion and passion will hurl you over whatever obstacle comes your way.

In his classic book *The Master Plan of Evangelism*, Robert Coleman said, "The criteria upon which any church should measure its success is not how many new names are added to the roll nor how much the budget is increased, but rather how many Christians are actively winning souls and training them to win the multitudes."[15]

CHAPTER 6

What's in Your Family History?

LIKE IT OR not, family history matters.

Every doctor visit starts out the same way: *please fill out these papers, and the doctor will see you in a few minutes.* I've learned over the years what they really mean is: *please fill out these same papers that you filled out last time while we try to find the doctor.*

I have filled out so many doctors' questionnaires over the years that it no longer takes long. After answering all the general questions, they want to know about my family history:

- Are your parents still living; and if not, when did they die?
- If deceased, how many years did they live, and what was the cause of death?

- Does (or did they, if deceased) your father or mother have high blood pressure, diabetes, hypertension, high cholesterol, short temper? (I just added that last one.)
- Have either of your parents had cancer, and if so, what kind was it? When did they have it? Where was it located?
- Do you have any siblings? If so, do they (or did they, if deceased) have high blood pressure, diabetes, hypertension, high cholesterol, sibling envy? (I added that last one too!)

Why does the doctor want to know so much about my family history? After all, I'm the patient, not my parents or siblings! The reality is that one's family history has a massive influence on a person's psychological and physical health. It can be a good indicator of how people are currently living and how they will continue to live.

In other words, if one or both of your parents struggle with high blood pressure, there's a good possibility that you will eventually struggle with high blood pressure. Or if one or both of them struggled with high cholesterol or diabetes or even cancer, there is a good chance you will too.

Family history matters—sometimes for the good and other times for the bad. Family history has a way of repeating itself and often prepares us for what is to come. For example, if both your parents died in their fifties due to heart attacks, that may be an indicator for you to get on a diet and exercise program early to increase the odds of surviving past your fifties.

Family History Matters

Family history not only can provide helpful information to explain physical attributes and challenges; it can also help explain our spiritual pilgrimage and current condition. Have you ever traced your spiritual heritage? It can be very enlightening.

I grew up in a Christian home to parents with similar spiritual backgrounds. On my mother's side, her grandfather (Big Papa, who stood 5 feet 4 inches and weighed in at 130 pounds) grew up Methodist, while her grandmother (Big Mama, who stood 5 feet 1 inch tall and weighed in around 100 pounds) grew up Primitive Baptist. He would drop her off at her church on Sunday and then make his way to his Methodist church.

My mother's mother grew up in the Christian church and became a Baptist in her fifties. My mother, who attended the Methodist church growing up, was never asked about her relationship with Jesus until she started attending an Independent Baptist church. That's when she personally met Jesus.

My father's family was a mix of Baptist and Methodist, mostly Baptist. When my parents got married, they started visiting a Southern Baptist church as a result of somebody from that church knocking on their front door, welcoming them to the neighborhood, and inviting them to church. That one knock on their door not only impacted the lives of my parents, it impacted my life and the lives of my children and grandchildren.

Family history matters! It gives us a glimpse into the past and helps explain the present. Consider the family history of Southern Baptists, a denomination born out of a passion and priority of evangelism. Included in the Charter of the Southern Baptist Convention, December 7, 1845, we read that it's purpose is for "eliciting, combining, and directing the energies of the Baptist denomination of Christians, for the propagation of the gospel."[1] *For the propagation* (which is defined in *The American Heritage Dictionary of the English Language* as "to increase or spread, as by natural reproduction) *of the gospel.*" Those assembled believed the unifying passion for Southern Baptists had been and should continue to be evangelism. They shared a common task: fulfilling the Great Commission of their Lord.[2]

The Southern Baptist Convention was born out of a hot passion for evangelism. For those of us in the Southern Baptist family, that is our history! Evangelism is in our DNA! Without the Great Commission (Matt. 28:19–20) there is no Southern Baptist Convention! It's part of our family history.

In 1945, the SBC baptized about 257,000 people. In 1955, the SBC baptized about 417,000 people. It took ten years to double our baptisms (1945–1955), making that the fastest decade of growth in SBC history. Since that decade the harvest has rapidly and consistently shrunk. According to the 2018 annual *SBC Book of Reports*, Southern Baptists baptized 281,000 people in 2016, which continues the longest decline in baptisms in our history.[3]

So, what's happened to us? Are we no longer as committed to the Great Commission as those who preceded us? How could we be baptizing fewer in 2017 than we did in 1955, with more seminary-trained ministers, more churches, more resources, and more opportunities? We currently have more than ever in our history, yet we are doing less with more! Does evangelism no longer characterize Southern Baptists? What about our history? What about our DNA?

Reversing the Baptism Decline

An amazing comparison in Southern Baptist life may shed some light on the decline in our baptisms. When the SBC began de-emphasizing the discipleship of believers, starting back in the late 1960s, the baptism decline began. According to Dr. Charles Kelley, "The most significant and influential death in the modern history of the SBC was the death of a strategic plan or template for discipleship in Southern Baptist churches."[4]

Renewed Emphasis on Discipleship

Southern Baptist history clearly indicates that we will not return to the priority of reaching people for Christ and baptizing them without a renewed priority on discipleship. When our discipleship efforts are strong, our evangelistic efforts are strong. When our discipleship efforts are weak, our evangelistic efforts are weak.

Discipleship is that process of becoming more like Jesus. It's what the Bible describes in Romans 8:29 as becoming "conformed to the image of his Son." The more like Jesus we become, the more soul conscious we become. The more soul conscious we become, the more burdened for souls we become. The more burdened for souls we become, the more we share Jesus with others. And it all starts with discipleship! If more of us looked and lived like Jesus, the more we would witness to others. As someone once said, "We have to first live a life worth sharing before we can share a life worth living."

It's time we Southern Baptists tapped into our DNA! If history does repeat itself, we desperately need it now. As our society continues drifting away from any resemblance of godliness, it's time we recaptured the passion and priority of previous generations in this matter of soul winning before it's too late.

Where do we start? What steps can we take to get back to the main thing of sharing Jesus and seeing people saved? How can we engage our church members in sharing Jesus with others? What can we learn from our Baptist family history to help us better reach this generation with the good news of Jesus?

To experience a fresh wind of God that engages believers in witnessing and helping lead others to faith in Jesus Christ we'll begin with a renewed emphasis on discipleship. In looking back at when Southern Baptists were seeing more reached for Christ and baptized, Dr. Kelley says, "Discipleship was actually the engine that pulled the train in SBC churches." Our Southern Baptist family history tells us that discipleship leads to evangelism that leads to New Testament growth.

Discipleship + Evangelism = New Testament Growth

When you remove discipleship from the equation, evangelism will decrease. When you include discipleship in the equation, baptisms will be increase. We are at our evangelism best when making much of discipleship. It really is that simple.

When I was growing up in a Southern Baptist church, attendance in Sunday evening Training Union was nearly as large as Sunday school. During that time we played Bible Baseball and learned about missionaries around the world and what it meant to live for Jesus. The focus was on discipleship—growing in our relationship with Jesus. But our SBC landscape has certainly changed.

There was a day in SBC life when at the Monday pastors' conference, the discussion was "How many did you have in Sunday school and Church Training yesterday, and how many were baptized?" Today we basically ask one question: "How many did you have in worship yesterday?" Sometimes the question is simply, "How many did you have yesterday?" And those involved in the discussion know that the question is about worship attendance.

Our metric for "a good day" has shifted from the number of participants in Bible study and discipleship and baptism to the number in worship. If you doubt that, let me ask you a question: When was the last time somebody asked you, "How many did you have in Bible study last Sunday?" or "How many did you baptize last Sunday?" We talk about things important to us. Our focus has definitely shifted.

Please don't get me wrong. I love worship, and worship should be done with excellence as we exalt the name of Jesus! But for the baptism decline in our churches to stop and reverse direction, we must have a renewed emphasis on discipleship—a kind of discipleship that leads to evangelism. Diminished discipleship leads to a decline in evangelism. The more we grow in our relationship with Jesus, the more like Jesus we become. The more like Jesus we become, the more we'll look like Him who "has come to seek and to save the lost" (Luke 19:10).

Greater discipleship produces a greater harvest of souls. Less discipleship results in a smaller harvest of souls.

Return to Evangelism Training

Our family history also tells us that a return to evangelism training will help reverse our baptism trends. C. E. Matthews, former Southern Baptist director of evangelism, said, "It is our tendency to move away from rather than toward evangelism." Much like a fire that starts out in a blaze and over time becomes just a flicker, if someone isn't there to fan the flame of evangelism, it never returns to a blaze. That's what evangelism training does: it fans the flame!

In 2016, the West Tennessee Evangelism Rally was launched on the campus of Union University in Jackson, Tennessee, for the purpose of encouraging and equipping believers in sharing Jesus. The rally consisted of a dozen breakout sessions covering a broad range of topics to help equip believers in sharing Jesus and then concluded with an inspiring worship gathering.

To our surprise, more than eight hundred people showed up for the event, and that number continues to grow each year. The main emphasis is training people how to share Jesus. This event has become so successful that now the Tennessee Baptist

Mission Board is starting similar events in Middle and East Tennessee.

Our members are starving for evangelism training. They need more than inspiration; they need training. Years ago, as a young pastor, I attended the Texas Baptist Evangelism Conference with fifteen thousand plus in attendance. It was an incredible experience listening to the finest preachers across the land. I couldn't take notes fast enough.

The only problem was that when the conference concluded, we all left on fire to share Jesus but no better equipped to get the job done. Too often the pastor challenges his congregation to share Jesus but neglects training them, leaving the members frustrated and feeling guilty.

Every church can provide evangelism training for their members regardless of size. Start with a one-day witness-training event, and watch your members become active in sharing Jesus. See how their worship becomes more vibrant having shared Jesus with someone during the week. Every church can train its members in evangelism, and every member can become active in sharing Jesus. More than likely the members will not initiate this; they need to be encouraged and equipped by church leaders.

A variety of evangelism training tools are available today for our churches: 3 Circles, Evangelism Explosion, People Sharing Jesus, CWT, The Way of the Master, Gospel Tracts, and more. Any of these could be helpful for your context.

Recognize the Principle of Sowing and Reaping

That leads me to a third step in reversing our current baptism trends: recognize the principle of sowing and reaping. Without the act of planting, there will never be a harvest. We read in Galatians 6:7–8, "Don't be deceived: God is not mocked. For whatever a person sows he will also reap, because the one who sows to his flesh will reap destruction, but the one who sows to the Spirit will reap eternal life from the Spirit." And we read in Psalm 126:5–6, "Those who sow in tears will reap with shouts of joy. Though one goes along weeping, carrying the bag of seed, he will surely come back with shouts of joy, carrying his sheaves."

> No farmer would anticipate a harvest without sowing seeds, and no church should anticipate a harvest without sowing gospel seeds.

Using the analogy of farming, we're reminded that before reaping comes sowing. No farmer would anticipate a harvest without sowing seeds, and no church should anticipate a harvest without sowing gospel seeds. The more seeds we sow, the greater the harvest we will have. Our current baptism trends indicate that most of our members are sowing few seeds throughout the week.

It all starts with church leaders, beginning with the pastor. Pastor, I plead with you to include witnessing throughout your weekly routine. If you're too busy to share Jesus, then you're too busy. Nothing is more powerful and encouraging to your members than when they hear you talk about a witnessing encounter you had during the week.

Years ago I heard a story told about a man who visited the local zoo one Saturday afternoon. As he came to the cage that housed the monkeys, he made an amazing observation. Whatever the little monkeys saw the big monkeys do, they would soon mimic. When the big monkeys swung on a limb, soon the little monkeys swung on a limb. When the big monkeys ate a banana, the little monkeys soon ate a banana.

We may not come from monkeys, but we sure act like them at times. We, like they, are hardwired to follow the example of our leaders. It's time for all the church's leaders to get busy sowing gospel seeds because when the rest of the church sees this, it's just a matter of time until they follow suit, which eventually will produce a harvest.

The principle of sowing and reaping reminds us that:

- We reap what we sow.
- We reap after we sow.
- We reap more than we sow.

Seedtime is always followed by harvest. As we recognize the principle of sowing and reaping, we are more apt to engage the lost with the gospel. We are reminded in Galatians 6:9,

"Let us not get tired of doing good, for we will reap at the proper time if we don't give up."

When the members of our churches begin following the example of the leaders and begin actively and consistently sowing gospel seeds, more people will be reached for Christ. Dr. Kelley in *Fuel the Fire* says, "To be an evangelistic church, sow the gospel and reap conversions." He goes on to say, "The critical question is: What is the church's present process for creating an evangelistic climate in the church, for sharing the gospel with people outside the church, and for cultivating and nurturing people who express openness to the gospel?"[5]

It's time for us to get back to sowing, so that we can get back to reaping!

"Jesus has placed the seed in your hand. You can either hang on to it, or you can sow it. There is only one wise choice."[6]

Reemphasize Church Membership

Another lesson we can learn from our Baptist family history to help reverse the trend in baptisms is reemphasizing church membership. Membership matters!

Mark Dever in *Nine Marks of a Healthy Church* lists five reasons "to join a church that preaches the Gospel and models Christian living."

To Assure Ourselves: That is to "help you in making certain that you are saved." He goes on to say that "church membership does not save, but is a reflection of salvation. In becoming a member of the church, we are grasping hands with each other to know and to be known by each other."[7]

To Evangelize the World: "Together we can better spread the Gospel at home and abroad. We promote the Gospel by cooperating to take it to those who have not yet heard it." We are better together. We can accomplish more together than separately.[8]

To Expose False Gospels: "As we interact with other Christians, we show the world what Christianity really is." Dever goes on to say we should "join with other Christians in covenanting to make the truth known."[9]

To Edify the Church: "A fourth reason you should join the church is to help in the edification or building up of other believers." Through the local church spiritual gifts are exercised for the building up of the saints.[10]

To Glorify God: "Our lives together are to mark us out as His and are to bring Him praise and glory."[11]

Over the last few decades, church membership has decreased as we have placed less emphasis and importance on it. In the average church, membership involves nothing more than filling out a card, giving a warm handshake, and being welcomed into the fellowship. In the current climate of decline in church membership, expectations have been lowered in hopes of experiencing an increase of membership. Ironically, lowering the bar of expectations has resulted in devaluing its importance and an even greater decline in its numbers.

It's time for us to raise the bar of expectations of church membership. At First Baptist Church in Cleveland, Tennessee, we are striving to make membership meaningful. Each member of our church is asked to invest at least three hours a week including worship, a small group, and service.

These are the expectations of members, and what we have found is that *the higher the expectations, the greater the engagement.*

There are many churches that require a personal interview with a staff member for anyone indicating the desire for church membership. The interview includes a discussion on their spiritual journey to ensure they have a personal relationship with Jesus Christ. In addition, the expectations of becoming a member are explained to potential members. Upon completion of the interview, the church votes to receive them as members during their quarterly business meeting.

Some churches require members, after an interview, to sign the church's statement of faith and church covenant. The Southern Baptist church I grew up in had a copy of the church covenant in every hymnal. Every time a worshipper reached and opened their hymnbook, there was no avoiding the church covenant that referenced various commitments church members made.

Jesus tells us in Matthew 16:18, "On this rock [Peter's confession in verse 16, "You are the Messiah, the Son of the living God"] I will build my church, and the gates of Hades will not overpower it." He didn't say, "I will build you a church," or "You will build you a church," or "You will build Me a church." Rather, He declared, "I will build My church!"

Jesus is building *His* church! He loved His church enough to die for it. How can we take lightly what was so costly to Him? Raise the bar! Membership matters!

It's true: family history matters! What does our family history reveal about our current situation and challenges? How can we learn from the genetic weaknesses of our family to make changes and at the same time perpetuate the great family legacy we have received?

CHAPTER 7

What Works Today?

DURING A RECENT eye exam, I heard the words: "You may want to consider bifocals." *Bifocals!* In case you don't know, bifocals are eyeglasses with two distinct optical powers. They are designed to assist those who have trouble seeing at a distance as well as up close.

I've gone through several stages over the years regarding my eyesight. I began wearing glasses in the fourth grade. In the seventh grade I began wearing contact lenses. In my early twenties I went back to glasses. In my forties I had LASIK surgery that was extremely successful. The only problem with LASIK surgery is that it only lasts for about ten to twelve years.

That brings me to today. To see clearly, my vision prescription now requires me to wear bifocals. To be completely transparent, the last couple of years, I've had to preach and teach without wearing my glasses in order to see my notes. The downside is that those I've been preaching to are extremely blurry! I hope my messages have been clearer to them than their faces have been to me! (The good news about this is that I've not been able to see if anyone is sleeping or dozing off during the message!)

But now, bifocals are coming! My vision will once again be 20/20! That will be a game changer!

What's true for my sight is true for our efforts in reaching people with the gospel: different times require different methods for maximum effectiveness. I could continue wearing my current glasses, enabling me only to see up close, or I could change to bifocals to maximize my sight. Likewise, churches can continue their current methods for outreach and evangelism with some effectiveness or change their methods to maximize their effectiveness.

Someone defined *insanity* as doing the same thing over and over expecting different results. The tragedy I see today is that many churches are choosing to die rather than to change their methods.

Let me say to every discouraged pastor and church leader: *your church doesn't have to die.*

Yes, our changing culture has created a need for new methods in sharing Jesus, but your church doesn't have to die or continue to decline! New methods for getting the gospel to your community may stretch you or perhaps make you feel a little uncomfortable, but won't it be worth it to see lost people come to know Jesus through the ministry of your church? Oftentimes changes that are needed to maximize our effectiveness in evangelism are not major changes but minor changes.

We've seen EE (Evangelism Explosion), CWT (Continual Witness Training), WIN (Witness Involvement Now), and others. It's time we see ECE (Every Church Evangelizing).

Every Church Can Evangelize

When the pastor says, "Let's do whatever it takes to bring our community to Christ," the church is on its way to revitalization, the lost on their way to being saved, families on their way to being restored, and the Lord on His way to receiving honor.

Every church can evangelize, including yours. Sadly, it can be easier to find a reason for not evangelizing than to find a path for evangelizing. "We're just too small," some may say. "We don't have enough money," or "Our members are too old."

The first church I served as pastor had recently renovated the Worship Center, painted, and installed new carpet throughout the buildings. They were proud of all they had done. But when I presented a plan to go door-to-door sharing Jesus throughout our neighborhood, they balked.

The prevailing attitude was, "Pastor, if we do that, the neighborhood children will come in and ruin all we've just remodeled and renovated. We've spent too much money on our buildings to see that happen." It's no surprise that the church later died.

It actually died years earlier; they just postponed the funeral.

But when the pastor says, "Let's do whatever it takes to reach our community for Christ," and the fellowship says, "Let's do it," that's a winning combination. When the pastor says, "Let's do whatever it takes to reach our community for Christ," and the fellowship says, "Let's not," that's a disastrous combination. Reaching communities for Christ requires both leadership and fellowship working together.

That leads us to an important question: *What works today in reaching the lost for Christ?*

I can tell you what doesn't work: not working! Getting the job done requires work and a lot of it. No longer can we depend on an "if you build it, they will come" mentality to reach our communities with the gospel. We need more "go and tell."

In 1 Chronicles 12:23, we read the beginning of the description of the massive army of David at Hebron: "The numbers of the armed troops who came to David at Hebron to turn Saul's kingdom over to him, according to the LORD's word, were as follows," and then comes the list of them by division and numerical strength:

From the Judahites: 6,800 armed troops bearing shields and spears. From the Simeonites: 7,100 valiant warriors ready for war. From the Levites: 4,600 in addition to Jehoiada, leader of the house of Aaron, with 3,700 men; and Zadok, a young valiant warrior, with 22 commanders from his father's family. From the Benjaminites, the relatives of Saul: 3,000 (up to that time the majority of the Benjaminites maintained their allegiance to the house of Saul). From the Ephraimites: 20,800 valiant warriors who were famous men in their ancestral families. From half the tribe of Manasseh: 18,000 designated by name to come and make David king. (vv. 24–31)

Then we come to verse 32: "From the Issacharites, who understood the times and knew what Israel should do: 200 chiefs with all their relatives under their command."

Here's what set the sons of Issachar apart from the rest of them: they "understood the times and knew what Israel should do."

While others had reputation and strength and might, the sons of Issachar were men of knowledge, wisdom, intuition, and influence who knew exactly what to do and when to do it. It's one thing to be equipped for war; it's another thing to devise a plan for war. Both are necessary for victory.

Because of the influence of the sons of Issachar, Israel avoided much heartache and turmoil. They understood their times and what Israel ought to do for victory.

Today's church is in need of some modern-day "sons of Issachar" so they can present the gospel in the most effective ways possible. We need people who understand the times— people who can interpret not only the Scriptures but society as well.

So, what works today? If you could consult the sons of Issachar Church Consulting Firm and ask them to provide a variety of tools that would assist you in building the kingdom of God through your local church, what tools would they recommend? I believe there are a few that are essential.

The Strategy Tool

A tool every pastor and church leader needs for building and creating an atmosphere of evangelism is a Spirit-infused *strategy.*

Many pastors are not strategic thinkers. That's not being critical, just honest. Most pastors are so overwhelmed with the daily and weekly responsibilities of preparing multiple messages (not to mention funeral and wedding messages), visiting members in the hospital, overseeing the budget, meeting with members, visiting prospects, planning and attending various standing committee meetings and special committees, evangelism training, staff meetings, deacons meetings, elder meetings, and representing the church at community events—to name a few—that few have any energy or time for strategic thinking and planning. As a result, strategic thinking gets pushed to the side for the urgent ministry needs of the moment.

There are always exceptions, but most pastors, for various reasons, are not strategic thinkers and planners. I often ask pastors what their strategy is for reaching people for Christ in their community, and the majority of them admit they don't have one. The synergy tool minus the strategy tool results in frustration among church leaders and produces minimal results. A lack of strategy nullifies any synergy created. Frankly, the strategy helps create the synergy.

What is strategy, and why is it essential? Strategy is a plan of action or policy designed to achieve a major or overall aim. Strategy is a master plan designed to achieve a short-term or long-term goal.

Using *the strategy tool* includes short-term and long-term planning. Someone has said that life is hard by the yard and a cinch by the inch. Strategic planning should begin with one short step and build from there.

For example, begin with a weekly evangelism strategy that may include a one-day witness-training event for church leaders. In addition, consider handing out a gospel tract one Sunday morning to those attending worship and rather than preach a normal message, walk them through the tract and then give an invitation for people to repent and be saved. What a great way to proclaim the gospel and at the same time train your members to use a tract to share the gospel. Encourage them to take the tract and share it with somebody this week like you shared it with them.

A weekly evangelism strategy may include giving a public invitation at the close of a service. That could include walking to the front, filling out a card, or meeting in a certain location after the worship service to discuss their decision. I recently gave a public invitation and asked those who desired to receive Jesus to stand up. To the surprise of many, a deacon and choir member stood up in addition to a college student. After the church affirmed them by a round of applause, I asked them to step forward as the music began, and they all did. Walking forward was the easy part; standing up was the hard part. There are many ways to give a public invitation, and a plan for the invitation should be included in the weekly evangelism strategy.

A yearly evangelism strategy is helpful. Keep in mind that we tend to move away from evangelism, not toward it. That's why every church should include in its yearly evangelism strategy events to fan the flame of evangelism in the hearts of the church members. That could include church-wide events like revivals, special seasonal events like Easter and Christmas, vacation Bible school, block parties, etc.

First Baptist Church in Cleveland, Tennessee, recently had a Discover First event after the morning worship service where we invited those who had visited the church over the last year, but never joined, to a free lunch with the pastor. Each table had a designated trained leader to help guide the conversation. The pastor gave a quick review of what it meant to become a member of the church and presented the gospel, and eight people prayed to receive Christ while many more joined the church.

The yearly evangelism strategy should include periodic evangelism training for the members. Consider providing various kinds of training quarterly or semiannually that include a one-day witness-training event, which could be on a Saturday morning or Sunday during the Sunday school hour or in place of the Sunday night worship service. The three- to five-year strategies may include a three- to four-day training event for participants to go out and put into practice what they have been learning.

Equipping events should be included in the evangelism strategy of the church. Consider training various groups within the church. For example, set a time to train deacons in evangelism, or Sunday school workers, or parents with small children who need help introducing their children to Jesus, or choir members.

The Synergy Tool

Here's a tool that belongs in the toolbox of every pastor and church leader and is helpful for any size church. What is *synergy*? *Synergy* has been defined as "the interaction or cooperation of two or more organizations, substances, or other agents to produce a combined effort greater than the sum of their separate effects."[1]

The word *synergy* comes from the compound Greek word *sunergos*. The word *sun* is defined as "together," and the word *ergos* comes from the word *ergon* meaning "to work." When those two words are joined together, *synergy* speaks of "working together." It speaks of cooperation, a combined effort.

> Without synergy, efforts and energy are wasted.

It's one thing to create strategy, but without synergy, efforts and energy are wasted. It's easier to create synergy with a strategy in place. With synergy in one hand and a strategy in the other, working together to get the gospel to others, people will be saved.

Though the word *synergy* is not found in the Bible, the concept certainly is. Solomon tells us in Ecclesiastes 4:9–12,

> Two are better than one because they have a good reward for their efforts. For if either falls, his companion can lift him up; but pity

the one who falls alone without another to lift
him up. Also, if two lie down together, they
can keep warm; but how can one person alone
keep warm? And if someone overpowers one
person, two can resist him. A cord of three
strands is not easily broken.

That's synergy! A combined effort will get more accomplished
than an individual effort.

Southern Baptists made that realization manifest in 1925
when they launched the Cooperative Program, which depends
on individuals, churches, state conventions, and SBC entities
cooperating, working toward a common goal of sharing the
gospel with every person on the planet.

Prior to 1925, each SBC entity made special offering
appeals to the churches. This method was referred to as the
"societal" approach to missions and resulted in severe financial
deficits, competition among entities, overlapping pledge cam-
paigns, and frequent emergency appeals, which greatly ham-
pered the expanding ministry opportunities God was giving
Southern Baptists. Some entities took out loans to cover oper-
ating costs until pledges or special offerings were received.[2]

Southern Baptists discovered "sanctified synergy" by
choosing to work together. Since then, they have learned that
more can be accomplished through a combined effort than
through an individual effort. It takes synergy to get the gospel

to every person on earth, and it takes synergy to get the gospel to every person in your community. We are better together!

The friends of the paralytic in Mark 2 understood the synergy tool. Without synergy, they could have never brought their friend to Jesus. Consider their synergy in Mark 2:1–12:

> When he entered Capernaum again after some days, it was reported that he was at home. So many people gathered together that there was no more room, not even in the doorway, and he was speaking the word to them. They came to him bringing a paralytic, carried by four of them. Since they were not able to bring him to Jesus because of the crowd, they removed the roof above him, and after digging through it, they lowered the mat on which the paralytic was lying. Seeing their faith, Jesus told the paralytic, "Son, your sins are forgiven."
>
> But some of the scribes were sitting there, questioning in their hearts: "Why does he speak like this? He's blaspheming! Who can forgive sins but God alone?"
>
> Right away Jesus perceived in his spirit that they were thinking like this within themselves and said to them, "Why are you thinking these things in your hearts? Which is easier: to say to the paralytic, 'Your sins are forgiven,' or

to say, 'Get up, take your mat, and walk'? But so that you may know that the Son of Man has authority on earth to forgive sins"—he told the paralytic—"I tell you: get up, take your mat, and go home."

Immediately he got up, took the mat, and went out in front of everyone. As a result, they were all astounded and gave glory to God, saying, "We have never seen anything like this!"

Consider the paralytic. In the middle of Jesus' message inside the house, verse 3 says, "They came to him bringing a paralytic, carried by four of them." The word Luke uses to describe this man's condition was a technical word used to describe paralysis from disease of some part of the nervous system.[3] He couldn't walk.

Don't miss this. This man who needed a change in his life had surrounded himself with friends with faith, friends who had a heart for God, friends who had a deep faith in God. This paralytic sought and established synergy through his friends.

Consider his friends. If the paralytic's synergy was found in his friends, the synergy of his friends was found in their faith. Verse 5 says, "Seeing their faith (the faith of the man's friends), Jesus told the paralytic, 'Son, your sins are forgiven.'" Let me tell you something about faith: faith is something that can be seen.

Jesus saw their faith. It showed up in their conduct; they *did* something. Everyone could see the friends' faith. Their faith was seen by bringing their paralyzed friend to Jesus.

Is your faith showing? Every attempt to help bring somebody to Jesus is an opportunity for our faith to show.

> Every attempt to help bring somebody to Jesus is an opportunity for our faith to show.

The text does not say, "Jesus saw the faith of the paralyzed man" and forgave and healed him. Verse 5 says that Jesus saw "*their* faith"—that is, the faith of his four friends!

Jesus saw the faith of his friends by bringing him to Jesus, and Jesus saw the faith of the paralytic in his willingness to be brought to Him by his friends.

Can't you hear those four friends talking over a cup of coffee discussing what they could do to help their friend?

"We've got to find a way to get him some better help than he's currently getting."

Another friend responds, "I think he's getting discouraged. We've carried him to every physician in the area, and none of them have seemed to help."

To which another friend says, "My neighbor told me this morning that Jesus, the carpenter's Son, arrived in Capernaum a couple of days ago. I hear He performs miracles, and our friend certainly needs a miracle. If we could find a way to take him to Jesus, perhaps He could heal him."

Finally, they say together, "Let's do it!" But as they found the house where Jesus was teaching, they couldn't get in. The house was so full of people listening to Jesus teach that there wasn't room to get their friend in.

These men wouldn't be stopped. One of them said, "If we could get him on the roof (no easy task) and make a hole big enough to lower him into the house, we could get him to Jesus." Notice the synergy in verse 3, "*They* came to him." Verse 4, "Since *they* were not able to bring him to Jesus because of the crowd, *they* removed the roof above him, and after digging through it, *they* lowered the mat on which the paralytic was lying." Verse 5, "Seeing *their* faith. . . ."

Four friends. Not three friends. Not two friends. Not one friend but four friends. It took four men working together (synergy) to help bring their friend to Jesus. It took all of them working together to bring this man to Jesus.

Note that when verse 3 says, "bringing a paralytic," the Gospel writer uses a present tense verb (*phero*), which speaks of continual action. It could be said this way, "bringing and kept on bringing the paralytic." In other words, they kept bringing him until they could get him to Jesus because he was unable to take a step toward God on his own. Not one step! He couldn't get to Jesus without them.

People scattered throughout your community cannot get to Jesus without you working together with others.

Synergy begins with one person committed to a cause who enlists another person who then enlists another person who can cooperate together to produce *a combined effect greater than the sum of the separate effects.*

You say, "I am all alone. Nobody in our church has a desire to get the gospel to our community for me to enlist." That's what the prophet Elijah thought too. He said in 1 Kings 19:10, "I alone am left, and they are looking for me to take my life." Oh really? You're the only righteous person left? You're all alone, and the work of God rests solely on you? I don't think so. In fact, I know so, and if you don't believe it, consider what God told Elijah in verse 18: "I will leave seven thousand in Israel—every knee that has not bowed to Baal and every mouth that has not kissed him."

There Elijah was, feeling like he was the only one left, and the truth was there were seven thousand more just like him.

Friend, God has not left you all alone to carry the evangelism burden for your church and community. There are many more just like you. They wear the labels of church members, church staff, deacons, pastors, directors of missions, state convention servants, and family members, to name a few.

Seek them, and you will find them. Take the initiative to enlist them and seek their knowledge. There are conferences to attend to equip and encourage your leaders in this matter of soul winning. There are books to read and then be taught that will fan the flame of evangelism in the hearts of your members. Other evangelistic pastors are waiting for you to ask them to invest and mentor you in this matter of getting the gospel to your community. We are better together! Create ways to work together to get the gospel to your community.

Under the lordship of Christ, decide to be like the "Issacharites, who understood the times and knew what Israel [you] should do" (1 Chron. 12:32).

The Systematic Tool

Maximizing our evangelism efforts will never take place without using the systematic tool. With the strategy and synergy tools in hand, the systematic tool helps drive the efforts in reaching people for Jesus.

The word *systematic* means "something that exists according to a fixed plan or system." Systems for working a plan are necessary to maximize those plans. Evangelism requires regular and routine effort and lots of it. Executing the short-term and long-term strategies requires systematically engaging the lost with the gospel.

Where do we start? A good place to start is those casual opportunities we have. As we live out our lives across our communities, we need to begin seeing people as Jesus sees people: lost, lonely, hurting, empty, and in need of salvation.

Our casual conversations provide great opportunities for sharing Jesus with neighbors, servers at restaurants, hairstylists, those who help with your grocery bags, gym members, people at their mailboxes, playground, ballpark, coffee shop, and everyone else you casually encounter throughout the day.

We're missing opportunities every day for sharing Jesus because we're not looking for them. The next time you go out to eat, don't see just a server; see a person God loves who needs to hear about Jesus.

There are also current opportunities. Every church has current opportunities built into its weekly calendar for sharing Jesus that are often overlooked for evangelism.

> The next time you go out to eat, don't see just a server; see a person God loves who needs to hear about Jesus.

When was the last time the gospel was shared during your Sunday school/small group class and an invitation was given to receive Jesus? What about during a choir rehearsal? What about during a worship gathering? What about during children's church and all those other ministries that are already in place? Every one of them is an opportunity for sharing the gospel and giving people the opportunity to receive Jesus.

Then there are created opportunities. Every church can create events for sharing the gospel. Created opportunities can take place within men's and women's events, Valentine's Day banquets, Easter celebrations, vacation Bible school, RA Racers, sports camps, summer camps, Upward Basketball and Flag Football, block parties, Independence Day, senior adult retreats, marriage retreats, neighborhood cleanup day, Veteran's Day, fall festivals, Christmas music presentations, and evangelism training classes. It's not unusual for somebody to be saved during an evangelism-training event. These and other initiatives that are only limited by our imagination are opportunities for sharing Jesus.

The four men who brought their friend to Jesus in Mark 2 had to use their imagination. Had they limited themselves to the conventional way of getting into the house (through the door), their friend would have never been healed and saved. They had to get creative. They had to use their imagination. Somebody had to say, "We can't get him to Jesus through the door. What are our options?" Somebody else had to ask the "what-if" question: What if we try bringing him through the roof? What if we get him up on the roof and then make a hole large enough to lower him down to Jesus?" Somebody had to say, "I think that'll work. I'll climb up there and make a hole, and then you three raise him up, and I'll grab him long enough for you men to join me. Together, systematically, we'll get him up here. And then together, we'll slowly lower him down into the house. We're going to get him to Jesus, for Jesus is his only hope."

Those four men used three tools to help bring their friend to Jesus: the strategy tool, the synergy tool, and the systematic tool, which resulted in their friend's being healed and saved.

Every church can evangelize, including yours, through casual opportunities, current opportunities, and created opportunities. Like someone once said, "Where there's a will, there's a way," and that includes evangelism.

Strategy + Synergy
+ Systematic
= Success

As times change, the way we approach people with the gospel must change as well. My single prescription glasses no longer allow me to see with clarity. It's time for me to change to bifocals in order to maximize my eyesight. Sometimes change doesn't have to be drastic to produce greater results.

May God continue to raise up pastors and church leaders like the Issacharites, who understood their times, with knowledge of what their church should do to maximize their efforts in reaching the lost across their communities.

CHAPTER 8

Getting the Church Back on Her Feet

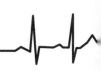

NO ONE RELISHES the thought of back surgery. It's generally the last and final option when someone has a severe back issue. Several years ago I blew out two discs and ruptured another one that literally put me out of commission. The pain was so extreme the hospital attendants had to carry me into the hospital from my car in preparation for surgery.

I remember lying in the pre-op room praying for God to miraculously touch and heal me so I wouldn't have to go through with the surgery. When the surgeon came into my room to describe the surgery, I asked him if there were any other options. "Ernest," he said, "there are no other options if you want to walk again pain free."

A few hours later I was in recovery hearing from my doctor that the surgery was a success. The celebration didn't last long because he then began describing to me the recovery process.

He explained that the next several months were going to be long and painful to get me healthy once again. He was right. Getting back on my feet took time, intentionality, and pain over the following several difficult months.

In the same way, developing an evangelistic culture doesn't happen *overnight*. It happens *over time* through strategic thinking and intentionality. The church that is not intentional about evangelism is unlikely to be evangelistic.[1] The church must first learn how to exegete its surrounding culture and context and then apply scriptural principles to that context. While the book of Acts is a great starting point, we must remember that some of what is described in the book is descriptive rather than prescriptive. We must look for underlying principles in God's Word and know when, where, and how to use them.

For example, Acts 12:24 says, "But the word of God flourished and multiplied." How did the Word of God continue to spread and multiply in the ancient context of the early church? Through free camel washes, Christian theater, or "bring a friend to the temple" day? Most likely not. While we do not know of the various strategies the early church used, we do know they focused heavily on personal evangelism.

But even the early church used attractional evangelism such as healings, miracles, and other events as platforms for evangelism. So it could not have been opposed to attractional evangelism. However, the focus of the early church seems to have been on unbelievers seeing a changed life and that changed person then telling unbelievers why they were changed.

J. D. Payne describes eight New Testament principles of personal evangelism as revealed by the early church:

1. They proclaimed an exclusive gospel.
2. They were intentional in sharing the gospel.
3. They were Spirit-led.
4. They understood the importance of culture.
5. They were flexible to the context.
6. They began where people were in their spiritual journeys.
7. They were sensitive to the fears, hurts, and concerns of others while speaking the truth in love.
8. They were post-conversion-oriented.[2]

Every church can create an evangelistic culture, including yours! It will not happen quickly, but it can happen with proper leadership and fellowship that is willing to follow.

The first church I mentioned earlier had 109 in Sunday school my first Sunday and had not baptized anyone in several years. Within the first year attendance was up to 160, and we baptized an average of one per month. That same year they gave more than $10,000 in one day to missions over against the $1,900 they gave the previous year. If that kind of spirit could prevail there, it can prevail where you are serving. With some patience, persistence, and planning, every pastor can help create an evangelistic culture in his church.

Getting a church back on its feet begins with a Spirit-filled, passion-driven pastor. A busy, frustrated pastor recently asked me how to keep the main focus on evangelism while meeting all the other demands and distractions of church life. Having served as a lead pastor for more than thirty-one years, I too know that frustration. I struggled having any energy or drive left for evangelism after seemingly giving it all toward shepherding the flock.

How do busy pastors and church leaders help create an evangelistic atmosphere and culture with all the challenges and distractions?

Priority

Sharing the gospel must be a priority in your life. Until that happens, creating an evangelistic culture in your church will be almost impossible. Jesus said in Luke 19:10, "For the Son of Man has come to seek and to save the lost," and then in Matthew 4:19, "Follow me, . . . and I will make you fish for people."

As we follow Him, we will fish for people. His followers are fishermen! We can fish without following Him, but we cannot follow Him without fishing.

I recently saw a man wearing a T-shirt that said, "The best way to catch fish is to fish where they are." Following Jesus increases our sensitivity and desire to go where the fish are so that we might see them caught.

I have found that the closer I walk with Jesus, the more like Jesus I become, and that includes witnessing. When evangelism is a priority in your life, it will eventually transfer into the lives of your church members.

Is sharing the gospel a priority in your life? Are you constantly and daily looking for people to share the gospel with? Do you see everyone as a prospect for Jesus? Are you praying and anticipating a divine appointment each day? A divine appointment has been defined as the following: *when a seeking soul crosses the path of a willing witness.*[3] That's a divine appointment, and God sends them our way every day. The problem is, those who don't prioritize sharing the gospel seldom recognize seeking souls because they are not looking for them. Every day seeking souls are crossing our path, longing to hear how they can have their sins forgiven and experience the grace and mercy of God. They are looking for a willing witness who cares enough about their soul and eternal destiny to tell them.

Is evangelism a priority in your life? I can tell you this: if evangelism isn't a priority in the life of the pastor, it is unlikely that evangelism is a priority in the life of the church. Creating an evangelistic culture begins in the heart of the pastor. I can tell you in five minutes if evangelism is a priority in your church with a quick glance at the church budget and calendar. The church budget and calendar reveal its priorities.

Practice

Sharing Jesus should become a part of your lifestyle. That's what Jesus was talking about in Matthew 28:19 when he said, "Go, therefore, and make disciples." We must share Jesus as we go!

Years ago I was invited by Dr. Ken Hemphill, who at the time was president of Southwestern Baptist Theological Seminary, to preach in chapel. After chapel, along with our wives, we went to a local restaurant for lunch. As the server brought our food to the table, they asked if we needed anything else. Ken answered, "Yes, there is. We're about to pray over our meal and were wondering if there is anything we can pray about for you today?"

Wow! I was blown away and at the same time thinking, *There's no way this server is going to give Ken something to pray about.* I was wrong! That server opened up to Ken about a family situation that really needed prayer. Immediately, Ken began praying before the server had time to walk away. As he prayed, he thanked God for the server and then asked God to give her wisdom in dealing with her family situation. Then he thanked God for her service to us and then for the food. As he concluded his prayer, I looked up, and to my amazement that server was still standing there with tears rolling down her face. Then she thanked him for his prayer.

That prayer changed my life. Since that lunch, I have made it my personal practice to ask servers what I can pray about for them. In addition to praying for them, as they bring me my ticket, I take a moment to thank them again for the privilege of praying for them and hand them a gospel tract about Jesus. I encourage them to take a few minutes during their break to read it and discover the steps to peace with God.

Over the years I've had less than a handful of servers turn down my offer. On one occasion I left the gospel tract on the table with a note to the server. As I was walking to my car, they ran out of the restaurant waving the tract shouting, "Thank you so much! This is exactly what I need!"

One day while having lunch alone, as is my practice, I prayed with the server and later shared the gospel with them. I didn't think much about it until Sunday during our deacons meeting. One of our deacons stood and shared how he saw me having lunch alone that day and admitted that he was watching to see if I really did that. After sharing with them what he saw, he said, "I'm glad that Ernest is our pastor. He practices what he preaches." That will go a long way in keeping evangelism a high priority while being pulled in different directions.

The Public Invitation

Inviting people to Jesus should become our practice. Not only individually but corporately. There may be a link between our decline of baptisms and the decrease of offering a public invitation during corporate worship.

Dr. Jerry Vines, longtime Southern Baptist pastor and leader, recently said, "Invitation is at the heart of the gospel. Those who respond to the 'Come' are to 'Go' and invite others."[4]

Dr. Jason Allen, president of Midwestern Baptist Theological Seminary, writes, "If you [the preacher] haven't invited, you haven't preached. If you haven't persuaded, you haven't preached. If you haven't begged, you haven't preached." He went on to say, "To be a preacher is to be a pleader, a persuader, a begger."[5]

The "invited," who have accepted God's invitation into saving faith, are called to become "inviters." When God said to Noah in Genesis 7:1, "Enter the ark, you and all your household, for I have seen that you alone are righteous before me in this generation," God extended a public invitation to him. When Jesus encountered the rich young ruler in Matthew 19:21, He said, "Then come, follow me." Jesus extended to him a public invitation to follow Him.

C. E. Autry, in his book *The Theology of Evangelism*, writes, "The primary purpose of the message of evangelism is to call men to a personal relationship with God."[6] He goes on to say, "If the church quits calling on people to decide, then death is certain. The church must never turn from inviting men to an encounter with Christ. The people of God have no choice but to keep a strong emphasis on confronting the lost, privately and publicly, with the gospel and calling on them to decide."[7]

Jesus tells us in Matthew 10:32, "Therefore, everyone who will acknowledge me before others, I will also acknowledge him before my Father in heaven." That certainly describes what takes place during a public invitation.

Moses invited people to decide. After the golden calf was destroyed, as he stood at the gate of the camp, he said, "Whoever is for the LORD, come to me" (Exod. 32:26).

So if giving a public invitation becomes a part of your evangelism practice, how should it be given after the proclamation of the gospel?

Give the Invitation Consistently

The late Charles Spurgeon is reported to have said, "Before you conclude any message, make a beeline for the cross." You never know whom the Spirit of God has led to attend any given gathering. They need to hear the gospel. And having heard it, they need the opportunity to respond.

When church members know what to expect when they bring their lost friends or family members, they are more apt to bring them. What a tragedy when lost people are brought to a worship gathering, hear the gospel message, and then walk out the same way they walked in: lost without Christ because they were never given the opportunity to be saved.

Consistently giving a public invitation will help create an evangelistic culture. It says to the members, "You can bring your lost family members and friends to worship here knowing they will be given the opportunity to be saved." As the public invitation is given and the church sees people coming to Jesus, you will be on your way to creating an evangelistic culture.

Give the Invitation Clearly

A clear invitation begins long before it's given. It begins in the study. In other words, the invitation must be prayed through and prepared for as much as the message itself.

Pastor and evangelist John Bisagno said, "Too often the invitation is thought of as unimportant, something that is tacked onto the end of a sermon." One day while I was visiting with Adrian Rogers about sermon preparation, he said, "Ernest, if my message has three main points, in my mind the fourth point is a carefully thought-through invitation. Never assume the hearers know what to do. You must explain what you're asking them to do."

It's not unusual for me after preaching a message to ask those attending to do one of three things. I'll say something like this: "First, some of you today need to come forward to receive Christ, and I'm asking you in a moment, when we stand to sing, to come forward, come see me, and say, 'Ernest, I'm here to receive Jesus.' (Oftentimes people need help in knowing what to say.) Second, I'm asking many of you today to use these next few minutes to pray about what God is saying to you. It may be about a sin in your life. It may be an obedience issue. It may be a relationship, finances, or health concerns. And third, I'm asking the rest of you to sing. Your singing is an encouragement to those around you. So when we stand, I'm asking you either to come forward to receive Christ, pray, or sing."

Often I say, "Please don't leave during the invitation. God is dealing with people all around you, and you don't want to be a distraction. So unless it's an emergency, and most things aren't, please remain in your place until after the invitation. I'd rather you leave before the sermon starts than to leave during the invitation and interrupt and insult the Holy Spirit."

Give the Invitation Creatively

There is more than one way to give an invitation. In the book *Preaching Evangelistically*, Al Fasol, Roy Fish, Steve Gaines, and Ralph West mention several ways to give an invitation, including: "Invitation to come forward, signing a card, counseling or inquiry rooms, lifting one's hand, praying where you are."[8]

I was in a worship gathering recently where the pastor asked those who would give their hearts to Jesus to stand and declare with their mouths, "I'm ready to go all-in with Jesus," and fifteen people stood! They were then invited to come forward, and the pastor prayed over them, and the decision counselors took them to a room for follow-up.

While I was serving as a short-term interim pastor at First Baptist Church in Clarksville, Tennessee, revival broke out resulting in more than thirty adults being saved over a three-week period. One Sunday a "stand to your feet" invitation was given and several stood, including a freshman student at Austin Peay State University, and a longtime deacon.

In following up with them on Monday, I asked them if they would be willing to join me on the platform the following Sunday and share what God had done in their lives. They agreed, so the following Sunday, there were three stools and microphones in place of the pulpit. When it was time to preach, I stood up and recounted what God had done the previous Sunday and that I had invited a couple of people to join me on the platform to share their story.

You talk about creating an evangelistic atmosphere! As they joined me on the platform, I thanked them for their courage and did a six-minute interview with each of them. I ended both interviews by asking them, "If you had one thing to say to those in attendance today, what would it be?" What a moment! The deacon looked toward the congregation and said, "I would say to you who know in your heart that you're really not saved, like I've been for years, to be saved today." The college freshman said, "I would say to you that have never decided to follow Jesus to decide to follow Him today. This past week has been the best week of my life."

When the invitation was given, a seventy-five-year-old deacon's wife and longtime member of the church came forward and took my hand and said, "Dr. Easley, I'm tired of being a fake. I need to be saved." In addition, four sorority friends who had been invited by the freshman girl who gave her testimony came forward weeping, saying they needed to give their lives to Jesus.

In that service those new followers of Jesus gave the invitation, and heaven came down! Be creative!

Give the Invitation Confidently

If you don't believe it, your hearers certainly won't either. As someone once said, "A fire must itself burn before it can give warmth to others." We are doing the Lord's business; therefore, we must not hesitate or apologize for it. We should just give it! Remember that we have the authority of heaven behind us as we invite the lost to Christ.

Give the Invitation Courteously

Our confidence, however, should never turn into arrogance. The invitation should always be courteous, never embarrassing the hearers but rather encouraging them. The invitation is a time for truth, not tricks; declaring, not deceiving.

Chuck Kelley, longtime president of New Orleans Baptist Theological Seminary, said, "Worse than being lost is being lost without anyone looking for you." The invitation to come to Jesus should clearly tell the lost that someone loves them unconditionally and is looking for them, and His name is Jesus.

Planning

Creating an evangelistic culture comes as a result of careful planning. That planning starts with the church calendar. If evangelism events and training don't make it to the church calendar, they probably will not happen. We calendar what we prioritize. What does your church calendar say about the importance of evangelism?

Included in your church calendar should be periodic witness training opportunities. As previously discussed, this could be a one-night, one-morning, or two-day event, or a weekly training to continue fanning the flame of evangelism, equipping your members, leaders, and new believers. Knowing that we naturally move away from evangelism, we need periodic events that help fan the flame.

Consider taking your leaders to an association or state convention evangelism conference or rally. Many associations and state conventions continue to provide innovative and practical evangelism training that are well worth your time.

Don't forget in your planning to include evangelism in your budget. The church budget should reflect a priority for evangelism. What are your church budget and calendar saying to the members about the priority of evangelism?

Promotion

Creating an evangelistic culture requires promoting it and keeping it in front of your members. That can be accomplished through witnessing testimonies during worship gatherings. Pastor Sam Greer at the Red Bank Baptist Church in Chattanooga, Tennessee, has his members text into the church on Fridays how many gospel conversations they had throughout the week and how many of them prayed to receive Christ. Then on Sunday morning he gives the church a report during their worship time where they celebrate together. What a great way to keep evangelism in front of the members, which helps create an evangelistic culture.

The ordinance of baptism is another opportunity for keeping evangelism in front of the members. Many churches prerecord the story of those being baptized and play it as a part of the person's baptism.

I recently baptized a family of five at First Baptist Cleveland, Tennessee, and told the story of how God used their eight-year-old son Patrick to help bring the entire family to Jesus. While at a park one day with his grandmother, he came running up to her and said, "Nana, I want to go to church Sunday. Will you take me?" The next Sunday they were all in worship for the first time. A few weeks later they all prayed and gave their hearts to Jesus.

As I told the story of eight-year-old Patrick and how God used him, the church erupted in applause. I cannot help but believe that other eight-year-olds in attendance that day thought, *If God can use Patrick to reach his family, then God must be able to use me to reach mine.* That's how an evangelistic atmosphere is created in the local church.

Backyard Bible clubs, block parties, mission trips, vacation Bible schools, and Upward sports events are all opportunities to keep evangelism in front of the members. I was in a discussion recently about the advantage of adding Upward Cheerleading to our existing Upward program. By doing so, we would have the opportunity to double our current participants, not to mention their families, allowing us the opportunity to get the gospel to them.

Not only by promoting various ministries, but also by reporting back to the church through videos, social media, and individual reports, churches can build evangelistic excitement and enthusiasm.

Churches have many ways to promote evangelism: vibrant worship gatherings, practical Bible teaching, and a warm welcome to those attending worship starting in the parking lots, to name a few. Everything the church does should be bent toward evangelism. Promoting evangelism shows it's a priority of the church and encourages members to get involved with sharing Jesus. Promoting evangelism also lets guests know that if they join your church, they are joining a church that is committed to sharing the gospel.

Conclusion

CONCLUDING A BOOK on evangelism is an oxymoron—
that is, a contradiction of terms—because biblical evangelism
never concludes; it continues. The work of the Holy Spirit in
spreading the gospel to the nations began in Acts 2 and continues today as He draws people unto salvation. God continues
allowing us to participate in the process of seeing people saved
through our walk and witness.

Resuscitation begins with perspective. There was a little
boy playing in the backyard with his baseball bat and ball. He
shouted, "I am the best baseball player in the world!" Then he
tossed the ball into the air, swung, and missed.

He picked up the ball, threw it into the air, and shouted
again, "I am the greatest baseball player in the world!" He
swung at the ball again, and again he missed.

He paused a moment to examine the baseball bat and ball
carefully. Then once again he threw the ball up into the air
and shouted louder, "I am the greatest baseball player who has

ever lived." He swung the bat as hard as he could and again missed the ball.

Not missing a beat, he then shouted, "Wow! What a pitcher!"

Perspective is powerful. It makes a huge impact on success or failure, including resuscitating the Great Commission in the local church.

In 2016, the North American Mission Board of the Southern Baptist Convention's *Your Church on Mission Blog* on February 2 posted: "What Are the Top Evangelistic Churches Doing That Mine Is Not?"

The blog revealed that only 26 percent of SBC churches were growing and discovered they shared three basic principles to reach people for Christ.

First, they had a pastor who led on mission. The number one factor for a church reaching people was the leadership of the pastor. Everything rises or falls on leadership, including churches. The blog stated that pastors who lead on mission have a vibrant vision, a simple strategy, and created a contagious culture. According to the study, in most of these churches, you can feel it when you walk through the door. There's something different.

Second, they gathered on mission. That is, they gathered with purpose and intent. They gathered around the gospel and engaged people with the gospel, and they expected to see people come to faith in Christ.

Third, the members lived on mission. They were living as missionaries where God had placed them, seeking opportunities to serve others and share Jesus. Once again: perspective!

Years after my father died, I came across his ninth-grade algebra report card from North Dallas High School in 1942. His attendance was good that year but not his grades. For three six-week periods when he received a grade, he received the same grade: F for failure!

How discouraging that must have been for him—showing up for class day after day, week after week, yet failing. As bad as that was, it got worse when he took his final exam. His grade for his final exam: G! When I saw that, my first thought was the same as yours: *What is a G, and how does anyone score a G on their final exam?*

On the back of the report card was the "Explanation of the Grading System." It started out normal:

A for Excellent

B for Very Good

C for Good

D for Fair

E for Poor Pass

F for Failure

Right under the "F for Failure" was the seventh group: G! Beside it as with the other grades was the explanation. I couldn't believe my eyes: Hopeless! My father's grade for his final exam was a G: Hopeless!

He probably wasn't surprised he made a G on his final exam. After all, his three Fs indicated he was struggling. But he didn't allow a temporary *hopeless* to prevent him from moving past it to success. After a brief time of serving overseas in WWII, he came back home and for more than thirty-eight years served as a branch manager lending money to people and eventually served as president of a bank.

You may look at your current situation and think, *This is hopeless! Nobody is being saved! It's been months since the baptismal waters were stirred. Nobody is joining our church. This situation is hopeless!*

Jesus didn't come to earth, die on a cross as a sacrifice and substitute for sinners, and rise on the third day for His church to be hopeless. His words to Peter confirm that: "I will build my church, and the gates of Hades will not overpower it" (Matt. 16:18).

It's time to move past hopelessness. It's time to resuscitate the Great Commission and return to our first love. Every person can reach somebody for Jesus. Every church can reach somebody for Jesus. Every person won to Christ adds not only to the membership of the church but also to the health of the church.

"Let us not get tired of doing good, for we will reap at the proper time if we don't give up" (Gal. 6:9).

Notes

Chapter 1: Checking Our Pulse

1. "New Study: Why Americans Are Dropping Out of Healthcare," Zocdoc, June 23, 2015, accessed April 21, 2018, https://www.zocdoc.com/about/news/new-study-why-americans-are-dropping-out-of-healthcare.

2. Lisa Robinson, W. Kip Viscusi, and Richard Zeckhauser, "Consumer Warning Labels Aren't Working," *Harvard Business Review* (November 30, 2016), accessed April 21, 2018, https://hbr.org/2016/11/consumer-warning-labels-arent-working.

3. David Jeremiah, "Seven Churches of Revelation Bible Study," accessed April 21, 2018, https://www.davidjeremiah.org/site/articles/seven-churches-of-revelation-bible-study.aspx.

4. Ibid.

5. George Eldon Ladd, *A Commentary on the Revelation of John* (Grand Rapids, MI: Eerdmans, 1972), 40.

6. Ernest Hemingway, *A Moveable Feast* (New York, NY: Scribner's, 1964).

7. Justin Taylor, "How Much Do You Have to Hate Somebody to *Not* Proselytize?," The Gospel Coalition, accessed October 30, 2019, https://www.thegospelcoalition.org/blogs/justin-taylor/how-much-do-you-have-to-hate-somebody-to-not-proselytize.

8. Chuck Lawless, "Introduction," in *The Great Commission Resurgence*, edited by Adam Greenway and Chuck Lawless (Nashville, TN: B&H, 2010), xv.

Chapter 2: Our Source of Strength and Power

1. Jennifer Riley, "Most U.S. Christians Don't Believe Satan, Holy Spirit Exist," The Christian Post, April 13, 2009, accessed February 5, 2017, http://www.christianpost.com/news.most-u-s-christians-don-t-believe-satan-holy-spirit-exist-38051.

2. Widely attributed to A. W. Tozer though there is no original source.

3. Stanley, Charles, *The Spirit-Filled Life* (Nashville, TN: Nelson, 2014), 20.

4. John Phillips, *Exploring Acts,* 40.

5. Charles Ryrie, *The Holy Spirit* (Chicago, IL: Moody, 1997), 183.

6. Billy Graham, *The Holy Spirit* (Nashville, TN: Thomas Nelson, 1988), 67.

Chapter 3: Addressing Malnourishment

1. Daniel Farr, "Malnourishment," in *Encyclopedia of Environment and Society*, edited by Paul Robbins (Thousand Oaks, CA: Sage, 2007), 1087.

2. Bill Hull, *Conversion and Discipleship* (Grand Rapids, MI: Zondervan, 2016), 20.

3. Barna Research Group, "New Research on the State of Discipleship," December 1, 2015, accessed November 1, 2019, https://www.barna.com/research/new-research-on-the-state-of-discipleship.

4. "New Research on the State of Discipleship."

5. Larry Osborne, *Mission Creep: The 5 Subtle Shifts That Sabotage Evangelism & Discipleship* (Hamilton, ON: Owl's Nest, 2014).

6. Robert Gallaty, *Rediscovering Discipleship: Making Jesus' Final Words Our First Work* (Grand Rapids, MI: Zondervan, 2015), 165.

7. Crystal Lombardo, "How Many People Die from Malnutrition Each Year," VisionLaunch, April 3, 2017, accessed November 1, 2019, http://visionlaunch.com/many-people-die-malnutrition-year.

8. Interview by Jessica Hanewinckel, "Michelle Sanchez: The Road to Missional Discipleship," Outreach Magazine, March 19, 2017, accessed April 23, 20180, http://www.outreachmagazine.com/interviews/21938-michelle-sanchez-2.html.

9. David Mathis, "Seven Costs of Disciple-Making," Desiring God, February 9, 2017, accessed April 24, 2018, https://www.desiring god.org/articles/seven-costs-of-disciple-making.

Chapter 4: Do Your Job!

1. R. T. France, *The Gospel According to Matthew* (Grand Rapids, MI: Eerdmans, 1985), 175.

2. Ed Stetzer, "Call Yourself a Christian? Start Talking about Jesus Christ," The Washington Post, May 19, 2016, accessed April 21, 2018, https://www.washingtonpost.com/news/acts-of-faith/wp/2016/05/19/call-yourself-a-christian-start-talking-about-jesus-christ/?noredirect=on&utm_term=.47c185d17585.

3. Chuck Lawless, *Nobodies for Jesus: 14 Days Toward a Great Commission Lifestyle* (Nashville, TN: Rainer, 2013), 3–4.

4. Chuck Lawless, "Nine Reasons Christians Don't Evangelize," Thom S. Rainer: Growing Healthy Churches Together, November 26, 2015, accessed April 25, 2018, https://thomrainer.com/2015/11/nine-reasons-cont-evangelize.

5. "Survey: Christians Are Not Spreading the Gospel," George Barna, November 30, 2017, accessed April 25, 2018, http://www.georgebarna.com/research-flow/2017/11/30/survey-christians-are-not-spreading-the-gospel.

6. "79% of Online Adults (68% of All Americans) Use Facebook," Pew Research Center, November 10, 2016, accessed November 3, 2019, https://www.pewinternet.org/2016/11/11/social-media-update-2016/pi_2016-11-11_social-media-update_0-02.

7. "List of Awards and Nominations Received by U2," *Wikipedia*, accessed November 3, 2019, https://en.wikipedia.org/wiki/List_of_awards_and_nominations_received_by_U2.

8. https://www.goodreads.com/quotes/tag/misattributed-mark-twain.

9. "Your Story Is God's Story: Creating Your Testimony," CRU, accessed March 18, 2017, https://www.cru.org/us/entrain-and-grow/share-the-gospel/evangelism-principles/how-to-tell-your-story-worksheet.html.

Interlude: The Pastor's Role in Leading an Evangelistic Church

1. Joel B. Green, *1 Peter* (Grand Rapids, MI: Eerdmans, 2007), 168.

2. Chuck Lawless, "Personal Evangelism and Pastors: Part One," Thom S. Rainer: Growing Healthy Churches Together, January 21, 2014, accessed April 25, 2018, https://thomrainer.com/2014/01/personal-evangelism-and-pastors-14-findings-part-one.

3. Martha Reese, *Unbinding the Gospel: Real Life Evangelism* (St. Louis, MO: Chalice, 2006), 9.

4. Mark Dever, "The Pastor and Evangelism," Desiring God Conference, February 3, 2009, accessed April 27, 2018, https://www.desiringgod.org/messages/the-pastor-and-evangelism.

Chapter 5: Overcoming Obstacles That Prevent Health

1. *The American Heritage Dictionary of the English Language.*

2. J. D. Greear, *Gaining by Losing* (Grand Rapids, MI: Zondervan, 2015), 26.

3. Ibid., 27.

4. Charles S. Kelley Jr., *Fuel the Fire* (Nashville, TN: B&H Academic, 2018), 33.

5. Tennessee Baptists' state paper, *Baptist and Reflector*, included this in "Worship Attendance Rises, Baptisms Decline in SBC Congregations" (July 11, 2018), 1.

6. Quoted in George Sweeting, *How to Witness Successfully* (Chicago, IL: Moody Press, 1978), 73.

7. Ibid.

8. Song "Do You Really Care?" by Broadman Press, 1967.

9. Quoted in Greear, *Gaining by Losing*, 146.

10. Scott Dawson, ed., *The Complete Evangelism Guidebook* (Grand Rapids, MI: Baker Books, 2006), 101.

11. John Dickerson, *The Great Evangelical Recession* (Grand Rapids, MI: Baker Books, 2013), 209.

12. Mark Dever, *Nine Marks of a Healthy Church* (Wheaton, IL: Crossway Books, 2004), 120.

13. Ibid., 119.

14. Kelley, *Fuel the Fire*, 145.

15. Robert Coleman, *The Master Plan of Evangelism* (Westwood, NJ: Revell, 1964), 104.

Chapter 6: What's in Your Family History?

1. This quote from the SBC charter can be located on sbc.net under "Mission & Vision."

2. Charles S. Kelley Jr., *Fuel the Fire* (Nashville, TN: B&H Academic, 2018), 10.

3. *Southern Baptist Book of Reports*, 84.

4. Kelley, *Fuel the Fire*.

5. Ibid.

6. J. D. Greear, *Gaining by Losing* (Grand Rapids, MI: Zondervan Publishers, 2015), 200.

7. Mark Dever, *Nine Marks of a Healthy Church* (Wheaton, IL: Crossway Books, 2004), 151–52.

8. Ibid., 153.

9. Ibid.

10. Ibid., 154.

11. Ibid., 159.

Chapter 7: What Works Today?

1. *The Oxford Dictionary*

2. This history of the CP is found on sbc.net under "The Cooperative Program" tab.

3. Herbert Lockyer, *All the Miracles of the Bible* (Grand Rapids, MI: Zondervan, 1961), 174.

Chapter 8: Getting the Church Back on Its Feet

1. Thom Rainer, "By the Numbers: What SBC Demographics Tell Us about Our Past, Present, and Future," in *The SBC and the 21st Century: Reflection, Renewal, and Recommitment* (Nashville: B&H, 2016), kindle edition.

2. J. D. Payne, "Eight Principles of New Testament Evangelism," Lausanne World Pulse Archives, May 2007, accessed April 29, 2018, https://www.lausanneworldpulse.com/themedarticles-php/700 /05-2007.

3. Darrell Robinson, *People Sharing Jesus* (Nashville, TN: Thomas Nelson, 1995), 26.

4. Jerry Vines and Jim Shaddix, *Progress in the Pulpit: How to Grow in Your Preaching* (Chicago, IL: Moody Publishers, 2017), chapter 10.

5. "FTC Workshop, Led by Allen, Focuses on Preaching," September 20, 2019, Midwestern Baptist Theological Seminary,

accessed November 6, 2019, https://www.mbts.edu/2019/09/ftc
-workshop-led-by-allen-focuses-on-preaching.

    6. C. E. Autry, *The Theology of Evangelism* (Nashville, TN: Broadman, 1966), 88–89.

    7. Ibid.

    8. Al Fasol, Roy Fish, Steve Gaines, and Ralph West, *Preaching Evangelistically.*